W9-ABK-792

# AMERICA
# GOD SHED HIS GRACE ON THEE

Robert Flood

————

illustrated by
Tom Fawell

moody press
chicago

*Printed in the United States of America*

To my wife, Lori,
and our son David Scott,
that he might understand
the true greatness
of America.

The Constitution and the Guerriere.

# TABLE OF CONTENTS

# INTRODUCTION

As the United States celebrates her bicentennial, many sense the groundswell of a major evangelical resurgence across the land. On college campuses, in many churches, in the corridors of the capitol, there is new spiritual excitement.

Behind the current evangelical "renaissance," whatever its extent, hangs a rich Christian heritage that few of today's generation understand. Are we really a "Christian" nation? If not, where *does* America stand? What did our forefathers really believe? And what difference does it make?

Already the bicentennial has produced no shortage of books that attempt to analyze the genius of America, and more will come. Some have tried to debunk men like George Washington, Thomas Jefferson and Benjamin Franklin. As far back as 1913 leftist-leaning Charles Beard wrote an economic interpretation of the U.S. Constitution that tried to undermine the founding fathers and portray James Madison as, philosophically, a Marxist, before Karl Marx was born! It was an audacious piece of historical deception, yet Beard's interpretations have dominated much of the teaching of history in American schools ever since.

Even some of the best books on our American heritage treat inadequately the evangelical dimensions, and many Christians today know amazingly little about the spiritual history of their land.

Today's happenings have their roots in the events of yesteryear. Yet this book is not simply a nostalgic excursion. We must know the past to understand the present, to clarify our spiritual identity and our origins. Such background can also help Christians anticipate the future. The revivals that shook our nation in times past can happen again. Such revivals provided the moral base for our nation to upright itself, and without this moral base, even a good democracy will eventually collapse.

In no way does this book pretend to be a complete course in American religious history. Its slant is distinctly evangelical, and at that it can only touch highlights. Many who would not be classified as evangelicals also played major

roles in the battle for religious liberty —among them even Thomas Paine and also the early Catholic settlers, especially in the state of Maryland. But hopefully this book has captured enough drama to give you a very real sense of God's sovereign hand upon the history of America.

The book is designed for those who are not ready to plow through heavy text material. With more than one-hundred-fifty carefully-chosen photographs and illustrations, it may be one of the most serious ventures into the field of visual-impact books.

The title may seem to declare that God has singled out America for special favor, or that He has put his stamp of approval on our nation *in toto.* The United States will be judged by God as severely as any nation which neglects Him. Other nations ultimately will prosper insofar as they acknowledge Him. God so loved the *world,* and his grace extends to all. The very word grace implies "unmerited favor." Yet America's spiritual foundations and her

evangelical thrust over two centuries bear directly, we believe, on the country's general prosperity and its position as a great world power.

I express special gratitude to Tom Fawell of American Motivate, Inc., who designed the graphics and who, as an American history buff, tackled this project with great enthusiasm. The continuity art is his, and also some of the photos. Others came from such photographers as Ake Lundberg of *Decision* magazine, Don Valentine of the Moody Institute of Science, *Moody Monthly* business and production manager Joe McKenzie and Dave Nystrom of the *Chicago Tribune.* Special credits go to Joe McKenzie, who spent much effort acquiring photos and art from across the country, and to *Moody Monthly* Managing Editor Jerry Jenkins, who did a superb job of final editing. An index of photos and illustrations, with their sources, is on page 192.

Robert Flood
Chicago, Illinois

CHAPTER ONE
# AMERICA—THE BOUNTIFUL

NO ONE IN THIS LIFE will ever fully know why it has pleased God to bless the United States of America with an abundance unprecedented in history, and with freedoms which are the envy of the world.

No, America is not perfect. She has scandals, unemployment, inflation, food and fuel "shortages" and pockets of poverty. There is even a crack in her liberty bell.

But half the world goes to bed hungry, and half the world also lies behind the Iron and Bamboo curtains where freedom, as Americans know it, just does not exist.

Homemakers in more needy parts of the world might never see in a lifetime the quantity of food from which the American housewife can choose in the course of her Saturday shopping at a supermarket. Many families enjoy large homes and cars, electric blankets and air conditioners, color TVs and stereos—as more and more luxuries become "necessities." The annual U.S. Gross National Product has now exceeded one trillion dollars!

In a book, *The Real America,* analyst Ben J. Wattenberg takes issue with those critics of our nation who see only her failures. He dispels the gloom with a wealth of encouraging facts—such as these:

Real family income, after inflation, has doubled in a generation.

In 1959, a fifth of all Americans were living in poverty. Now the total is half that.

College enrollment in 1960 was more than 3.6 million. By 1973 it had reached 8.6 million.

Americans now start working later, put in fewer hours and retire earlier.

And in a recent magazine article, "Let's Dispel the Gloom," world

Evidence of abundance: a typical U.S. supermarket

traveler Lee Braxton finds an attitude abroad that disputes the image of *The Ugly American.*

"In most countries I have visited," he says, "a taxi driver has asked such questions as, 'Would you be willing to take me to America?' or 'Will you guarantee me a job for so many months so I can go to America?'

"Some say that the whole world distrusts an American. I do not believe this. If this were true, would America continue to be the magnet that draws more immigrants from other countries than any other nation? And would more than 130,000 students leave their countries and homes to attend universities in America?"

Americans too often take for granted their affluence and their freedoms—

until perhaps they see firsthand one of the deplorable poverty areas of the world, or until someone from the "outside" speaks up.

Someone, for instance, like Polish immigrant Janina Atkins, who expressed her conviction in an article labeled "God Bless America," which appeared earlier in this decade on the editorial page of the *New York Times.*

"Just over six years ago," she wrote, "I came to this country with $2.60 in my purse, some clothes, a few books, a bundle of old letters, a little eiderdown pillow.... I was an immigrant girl hoping for a new life and happiness in a strange new country.

"There is something in the air of America that filled my soul with a feeling of independence, and indepen-

**There is something in the air of America that filled my soul with a feeling of independence, and independence begot strength.**

dence begot strength. There is no one here to lead you by the hand, but also no one to order you about ... we believed in the future. And the future did not disappoint us.

"Today ... my husband is studying for his doctorate. We live in a comfortable apartment in mid-Manhattan. Weekends we drive to the country....

"I love this country because when I want to move from one place to another I do not have to ask permission. Because when I want to go abroad I just buy a ticket and go.

"I love America because when I need a needle I go to the nearest Woolworths.... I love it because I do not have to stand in line for hours to buy a piece of tough, fat meat. I love it because, even with inflation, I do not have to pay a day's earnings for a small chicken.

"I love America because America trusts me. When I go into a shop to buy a pair of shoes I am not asked to produce my identity card. I love it because my mail is not censored. My phone is not tapped. My conversation with friends is not reported to the secret police.

"Sometimes when I walk with my husband through the streets of New York, all of a sudden we stop, look at each other and smile and kiss. People think we are in love, and it is true. But we are also in love with America ... standing in the street, amidst the

Chicago Skyline at night

noise and pollution, we suddenly realize what luck and joy it is to live in a free country."

THE PRIVILEGES WE ENJOY should make us stop to think.

Is this freedom and our abundance ours merely by chance?

Is it wholly due to what we like to think of as U.S. energy and know-how?

And are we in danger of suddenly losing the blessings we have so long enjoyed?

If God indeed has blessed America, why? What clues can we find as we examine some of the remarkable events and forces that helped shape the foundations of this nation?

Has the land itself made America great?

One of our most moving patriotic hymns reminds us of the beauty of America—a beauty that all who have traveled across the continent surely recognize. Katherine Lee Bates stood atop Pike's Peak and scanned the sweep of the land, then wrote of the purple mountain majesties, and the amber waves of grain. She concluded that God had shed his grace on this land—a vast unexplored wilderness that, in an astonishingly short period, grew into a great nation.

It would be foolish to deny that the rich natural resources of the land itself

The author's son in a field of grain near Paso Robles, Calif.

did not help to make her great. The oil, the ore, the timber, the water, the soil and climate, all combined to nourish a civilization that would eventually spread from sea to shining sea.

Other nations, too, have been blessed with fine resources; yet somehow these have not risen to such greatness.

Others have said that her people have made America great. Lyman Abott once said:

"A nation is made great, not by its fruitful acres, but by the men who cultivate them; not by its great forests, but by the men who use them; not by its mines, but by the men who build and run them. America was a great land when Columbus discovered it; Americans have made of it a great nation."

And so they have. For they pioneered a continent, subdued the elements that at first worked against them, molded a society of peoples from all over the world. America's initiative and ingenuity is known across the earth. Other nations have looked on in awe at her ability over the decades to produce not only her own needs, but much more.

Consider just her output of food supply.

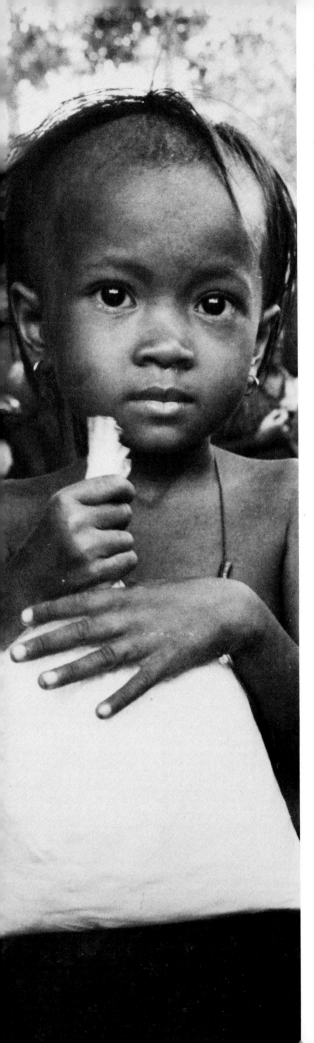

Hunger stalks most of the world

## Does material abundance of itself produce the kind of national character that counts most?

"Within your lifetime," declares a report in *Reader's Digest,* "American agriculture has advanced more than in all the preceding millenniums of man's labor on the land."

Before the Civil War, the American farmer produced food and fiber enough to feed and clothe himself and three other persons. A century later, after World War II, new machines and techniques had helped move that figure to himself and 11. Today it has leaped to himself and 42!

As a farm boy who first trained for a career in agricultural journalism, I saw a bit of this revolution firsthand. I remember when my stepfather sold his Caterpillar D-4 tractor for a model D-6 that would do twice as much work, and when he began to fertilize his grain to increase the yields.

At that time most of California's fruits and vegetables were hand-picked. Today machines can harvest even the most delicate crops. For example, a literal "factory-on-wheels" now moves down celery rows—severing, trimming, washing, crating, doing the work of 40 men. Today more than 90 percent of that state's tomato crop is picked mechanically. And much more may come—such as the largescale conversion of sea water for home and industry.

If the agricultural revolution has only just begun, the coming revolution in transportation could be even more dramatic. Out of the U.S. in decades past came such great inventions as the telephone, the radio, television, the airplane. Planners now foresee automated cars, automated highways and unbelievably rapid underground "tube trains" that could handle both commuter and long-distance passengers. The tube train, suspended and propelled by compressed air, may someday carry passengers on intercity trips at 350 miles an hour. On coast-to-coast runs it could conceivably become supersonic, sending riders by underground tunnel from the West coast to New York in only two hours!

AMERICA'S FREE ENTERPRISE system and the spirit of her people, it would seem, have combined to deliver a flood of mass-produced goods to the consumer at relatively low cost. Even energy shortages call forth the best elements of American ingenuity.

At the same time, American economic genius has also produced millions of jobs—from the factories to the professions—which give Americans the income to buy the goods they produce. Contrast this with a country like India, where production falls far short of need, and where, even worse, per capita income is only $79 a year!

But a nation which has flourished faces deep issues which, ironically, stem directly from her prosperity:

Does material abundance of itself produce the kind of national character that counts most?

How will the "have-not" nations react in the immediate years ahead?

What are our responsibilities in a world where want is known by millions?

Oregon's Senator Mark O. Hatfield, a man of strong Christian conscience, says "no problem is more likely to breed instability and conflict, and increase the magnitude of mankind's suffering in the years directly ahead, than the shortage of food."

We have already seen the effects of this in the Sahel region of Africa, where the Sahara Desert has expanded southward thirty miles each year during the current drought. Hundreds of thousands there have died of starvation.

Should affluent Americans feel guilty over this disparity? Some say yes, and point to the many Scriptures that clearly reveal an obligation to the poor. Others say no. It is impossible for American to feed the world, many point out, and the crisis can never be solved until other nations put free enterprise into action and remove some of the faulty religious foundations that have helped to create their own catastrophes. Both sides make a point, and the real answer probably lies somewhere in between.

**In an astonishingly
short period a vast
unexplored wilderness
grew into a great nation**

Thus far America has escaped the spectre of widescale hunger at home, and she has been able to feed at least some of the hungry abroad. Through the decades she has opened her heart to the poor of the world. She has given generously to every nation, even her enemies, in time of emergency. In 1974 the people of the United States gave 7.6 billion dollars to charitable, religious and philosophic causes.

In spite of social ills, the U.S. has passed more social legislation and enacted more laws providing individual liberty than any other nation in world history. And because of her belief in freedom of speech she has not hidden her scars—they are there for the world to see—while those totalitarian regimes that run a controlled press look on amazed.

All of these blessings point back to her foundations, and this connection becomes more clear in the pages to come.

In God's providence the U.S. has also been spared the agony of war with a foreign power on American soil. I was just a boy in California when the sudden Japanese attack on Pearl Harbor occurred only two thousand miles west out in the Pacific. How well I recall the school air raid alerts ... the frequent

pages 20-21, The forests of western Oregon

"blackouts" at night, when shades had to be drawn to conceal our city from possible attack by enemy planes ... and the brilliant searchlights that criss-crossed the dark sky. I had all but psyched myself up for the impending enemy attack. But it never came. One Japanese ship maneuvered close enough to lob a shell or two onto the U.S. mainland north of Santa Barbara. But the explosives fell harmlessly onto a remote section of coastline.

And so although the nation once saw a terrible civil war, and wars abroad have interrupted her history and cost her dearly, Americans at home have continued to build a nation without foreign invasion. And the United States achieved a position of prestige, world power and accomplishment unparalleled in history.

LIKE NO OTHER NATION America over the decades became a "melting pot" for the peoples of the world, and the extent to which millions even today seek freedom within our shores speaks loudly against our critics. Those who have known persecution in other lands know best what the United States and its liberties truly mean.

In an eloquent piece of prose, Rabbi Abba Hillel Silver saw—beyond America's natural resources and her people—the hand of God when he wrote:

"God built him a continent of glory, and filled it with treasures untold. He studded it with sweet-flowering fountains, and traced it with long-winding streams. He carpeted it with soft-rolling prairies, and columned it with thundering mountains. He graced it with deep-shadowed forests, and filled them with song.

"Then He called unto a thousand peoples, and summoned the bravest among them. They came from the ends of the earth, each bearing a gift and a hope. The glow of adventure was in their eyes, and in their hearts the glory of hope.

"And out of the bounty of earth, and the labor of men; out of the longing of heart, and the prayer of souls; out of the memory of ages, and the hopes of the world, God fashioned a nation in love, and blessed it with purpose sublime.

"And they called it America."

It was not a Gentile who wrote these words, but one whose strong sympathies for a "chosen land" might have been expected to lie, instead, with Israel.

With proper respect for the other nations and tribes of earth, Americans can still sing in good conscience, "America, America, God shed his grace on thee...." After all, the purple mountain majesties and the fruited plains originated with God. America's blessings,

earl Harbor: an attack that fell short of the mainland.

despite her ills, surpass the nations of earth and call forth thanksgiving from all those who enjoy them. The great spiritual heritage that built America unfolded by remarkable design. So also did American democracy, the U.S. Constitution and, along with these, the great freedoms they assure.

No, America did not just happen by chance, as is obvious to a person who truly understands the unfolding saga of events that shaped this nation. The pages that follow highlight some of this evidence, not that we should simply look back, but that we should better understand where America is today, how she arrived here, and where she must turn at this critical hour.

For as Thomas Jefferson once asked, "Can the liberties of a nation be thought secure, when we have removed their only firm basis, a conviction in the minds of the people that these liberties are the gift of God? That they are not to be violated but by his wrath? Indeed, I tremble for my country when I reflect that God is just; that his justice cannot sleep forever."

CHAPTER TWO

# LAND ACROSS THE SEA

MANY OF THE MOST DRAMATIC events of history have unfolded on the high seas. The oceans breathe excitement, and often so do the ships and the men who sail them. Great naval battles—even the sinking of a single ship like the *Bismarck*—have suddenly changed the directions of wars. The seas can be tragic in death, or beautiful in victory. Ocean waters swallowed the *Titanic,* but they also absorbed the impact of our astronauts as they returned from the moon.

In the Bible, too, are sea conflicts. The apostle Paul, in his relentless pursuit to spread the gospel to the ends of the then-known world, suffered shipwreck more than once. In Acts 27 he describes with great vividness a harrowing experience off the island of Malta. The action of that chapter equals the greatest of sea dramas.

The disciples fought for their lives in a sudden furious storm upon the sea of Galilee—until the Master of oceans and earth and skies commanded, "Peace, be still."

The sea and its dangers have inspired countless analogies in our hymns and gospel songs. Writers have warned of the shoals, waves and billows in "life's tempestuous sea," and at the same time have pointed to Jesus as "the Pilot" and "the Anchor" that holds.

At least three great sea dramas set the stage for the emergence of the American nation. Every school-child has read the historical facts, but few Americans know the real stories, or the full Christian significance, that lay behind each of these events.

CHRISTOPHER COLUMBUS, say most of the history books, discovered the New World. Not everyone thinks so. Nordic mariner Leif Ericson, some insist, arrived first. Others cite a nautical chart, lost for five centuries,

## Columbus was a devout man with a sense of destiny.

which gives evidence that Portuguese captains had found the New World by 1424. And there are at least a score of other speculations.

The debate may never be resolved. But one thing is sure: Columbus was one of the great seamen of all time. As a young lad, while employed making charts and sailing up and down the coasts of Europe and Africa under the Portuguese flag, he began to dream of the "impossible trip."

By this time every educated man knew the world was a sphere. And so they also understood that, theoretically, it would be possible to reach the Orient and its rich trade potential by sailing west. But no one had the courage to prove it. To the west lay a dark, turbulent waste, and who knew how far it might stretch? Little did they suspect that still another continent lay between!

Columbus borrowed from Marco Polo some calculations on the size of China and Japan, and a faulty estimate on the size of Asia from Marinus of Tyre. He then underestimated the length of a degree, which made the earth about one-sixth smaller than actuality.

It took Columbus years to gain support for his idea of sailing west, and then to raise the finances for the actual voyage. Queen Isabella of Spain, impressed with Columbus as a person and aware of what the expedition's success could mean to Spain, finally granted the funds.

Columbus elected to put together a small fleet of three ships, mainly so that if one sank, two would still be near for the rescue. Columbus pushed off from Lisbon, choosing first to run south before the prevailing northerlies to the Canary Islands. There the ships stopped for food and repairs, weighed anchor for the last time in the Old World and headed due west into the dark unknown. On September 6 they passed the lofty 12,000-foot peak of Tenerife in the Canary Islands, which remained in sight until September 9.

**By the nightfall of September 9, every trace of land had sunk below the eastern horizon.**

But by nightfall that day, every trace of land had sunk below the eastern horizon, and the three ships were alone on an unchartered ocean. Columbus described the course: "West; nothing to the north, nothing to the south."

What really motivated this great explorer to sail off into uncharted waters? Historians have often summed up the early migrations to America as ventures for "God, gold and glory." Where, then, did this man's greatest interests lie?

The Sovereigns who underwrote the voyage promised Columbus a healthy ten percent of the expected profits. But this was not an unusual amount at that time, nor did the profit motive seem to preoccupy him. Some of his ships' crew perhaps, but not so Columbus himself.

Then it must have been the adventure and glory that impelled him. Columbus indeed was equal to the adventure of all adventures, and surely he knew the honors that would be his if he returned home in success.

But was this the whole picture?

Even secular historians acknowledge that Columbus was a devout man with a sense of destiny. But for the most part they have missed or underplayed the greatest single driving force behind the voyage of Columbus: the impact of the Bible upon his life.

August J. Kling, who has researched the subject thoroughly, says that "Col-umbus' use of the Bible is one of the best documented facts of his remarkable career, but it is one of the least known to the general public."

Christopher Columbus, he says, was a careful student of the Scriptures and of great biblical commentators to which he had access. He used Latin fluently and knew enough elementary Greek and Hebrew to study the exegesis of certain biblical words that were of special interest to him.

For his time he was an unusual self-taught Christian layman. "All of Columbus' sailing journals and most of his private letters," observes Kling, "give evidence of his biblical knowledge and his devout love for Jesus Christ."

At this point some will object that Columbus lived under the theology of the Roman Church and, indeed, was loyal to it.

But remember, this was still a quarter century before the Reformation, and even our own "evangelical ancestry" lived under the same umbrella. It would have been impossible, then, for Columbus to be a Protestant!

But let Columbus tell the story in his own words. They are translated from the fifteenth century Spanish introduction to the *Book of Prophecies,* the least known of Columbus' endeavors, yet the only book he ever wrote. Here are some excerpts:

"At a very early age I began to sail

upon the ocean. For more than forty years, I have sailed everywhere that people go.

"I prayed to the most merciful Lord about my heart's great desire, and He gave me the spirit and the intelligence for the task: seafaring, astronomy, geometry, arithmetic, skill in drafting spherical maps and placing correctly the cities, rivers, mountains and ports. I also studied cosmology, history, chronology and philosophy.

"It was the Lord who put into my mind (I could feel His hand upon me) to sail from here to the Indies. All who heard of my project rejected it with laughter, ridiculing me. There is no question that the inspiration was from the Holy Spirit, because he comforted me with rays of marvelous illumination from the Holy Scriptures ... encouraging me continually to press forward, and without ceasing for a moment they now encourage me to make haste.

"It is possible that those who see this book will accuse me of being unlearned in literature, of being a layman and a sailor. I reply with the words of Matthew 11:25: 'Lord, because thou hast hid these things from the wise and prudent, and hast revealed them unto babes.'

"The Holy Scripture testifies in the Old Testament by the prophets and in

**Secular historians have underplayed the greatest single driving force behind the voyage of Columbus.**

the New Testament by our Redeemer Jesus Christ, that this world must come to an end. The signs of when this must happen are given by Matthew, Mark and Luke. The prophets also predicted many things about it.

"Our Redeemer Jesus Christ said that before the end of the world all things must come to pass that had been written by the prophets. Isaiah goes into great detail in describing future events and in calling all people to our holy catholic faith."

At least one secular writer has suggested that Columbus, as a geographer of vision, might also have been inspired by Psalm 19, or Ezekiel's reference to "the isles that are in the sea" or to Psalm 72:8—"Ye shall have dominion also from sea to sea, and from the river unto the ends of the earth."

But more from Columbus:

"I am a most unworthy sinner, but I have cried out to the Lord for grace and mercy, and they have covered me completely. I have found the sweetest consolation since I made it my whole purpose to enjoy His marvelous presence.

"No one should fear to undertake any task in the name of our Saviour, if it is just and if the intention is purely for His holy service. The working out of all things has been assigned to each person by our Lord, but it all happens according to His sovereign will, even though He gives advice. He lacks nothing that

it is in the power of men to give him. O what a gracious Lord, who desire that people should perform for Him those things for which He holds Himself responsible! Day and night, moment by moment, everyone should express to Him their most devoted gratitude.

"These are great and wonderful things for the earth, and the signs are that the Lord is hastening the end. The fact that the gospel must still be preached to so many lands in such a short time—this is what convinces me."

ONE WONDERS IF when the ocean waters churned at their worst and his crew threatened mutiny, Columbus would have made it had he not been driven on by his strong sense of divine mission and destiny.

Only three days away from their landing, his men demanded in anger that the ships turn back. They had not seen land for thirty-one days. Enough of this nightmare to nowhere! But Columbus, in determination, urged them on, with the cry of *Adelante! Adelante!* ("Onward") since he "had come to go to the Indies, and so had to continue until he found them, with Our Lord's help."

Some years ago this example of a man who wouldn't quit inspired American poet "Joaquin" Miller to write the following now famous account, "Columbus":

# Sail On! Sail On!

Behind him lay the gray Azores,
    Behind the Gates of Hercules;
Before him not the ghost of shore,
    Before him only shoreless seas.
The good mate said: "Now must we pray,
    For low! the very stars are gone.
Brave Adm'r'l, speak; what shall I say?"
    "Why, say: 'Sail on! sail on! and on!'
"My men grow mutinous day by day;
    My men grow ghastly wan and weak."
The stout mate thought of home; a spray
    Of salt wave washed his swarthy cheek.
"What shall I say, brave Adm'r'l, say,
    If we sight naught but seas at dawn?"
"Why, you shall say, at break of day:
    'Sail on! sail on! sail on! and on.' "

They sailed and sailed, as winds might blow,
    Until at last the blanched mate said:
"Why, now not even God would know
    Should I and all my men fall dead.
These very winds forget their way,

For God from these dread seas is gone.
Now speak, brave Adm'r'l; speak and say"—
    He said: "Sail on! sail on! and on!"

They sailed. They sailed. Then spake the mate:
    "This mad sea shows his teeth to-night;
He curled his lips, he lies in wait,
    With lifted teeth, as if to bite:
Brave Adm'r'l, say but one good word;
    What shall we do when hope is gone?"
The words leapt like a leaping sword:
    "Sail on! sail on! sail on and on!"

Then, pale and worn, he kept his deck,
    And peered through darkness. Ah, that night
Of all dark nights! And then a speck—
    A light! a light! a light! a light!
It grew, a starlit flag unfurled!
    It grew to be Time's burst of dawn.
He gained a world; he gave that world
    Its grandest lesson; "On! sail on!"

No, even in their darkest hour, "God from these dread seas" was *not* gone. Like the disciples on the tumultuous sea of Galilee and Paul in the terrifying storm off Malta, Columbus saw that "the Lord on high is mightier than ... the mighty waves of the sea" (Ps. 93:4).

Obviously, Columbus saw the success of his voyage as a direct confirmation of God's will for his life. He saw his discovery as opening up new lands and tribes to the gospel. And he understood something of how the missionary task—the preaching of the gospel to the ends of the earth—related to prophecy.

Columbus named his first landfall "San Salvador" (Holy Savior). And in February, 1502, while preparing for his fourth voyage, he asked for clergymen to assist him, "in the name of the Lord

**Columbus saw the success of his voyage as a confirmation of God's will for his life**

Jesus to spread his name and Gospel everywhere." Columbus specified that he wanted to select these evangelists himself.

In this ultimate mission, however, he was to face disappointment. Writes

Kling: "The soldiers and adventurers who followed him in later voyages to the new world had little interest in missionary work, in Bible studies or in the preaching of the gospel."

In retrospect, it was fortunate that such a spread of the gospel awaited another century or more—until the Reformation had exploded in southern Europe, spread northward to the British Isles, then jumped across the sea to the North American shore. By this time the "gospel" had been purged of the faulty and extraneous trappings which had prompted the furious Martin Luther to hammer his 95 Theses to the door at Wittenburg.

Though Columbus may have failed in his own long-range goal, he attained "the dark continent." And because of this, he returned a hero to his country-

men, to the world of that time, and to the billions who would read about him in the annals of history.

THE DEFEAT OF THE SPANISH ARmada stands as a second pivotal high sea event that helped shape the Christian face of North America.

On a July evening in 1588, Spain's "invincible" fleet of one hundred thirty ships churned through the English Channel with 30,000 men aboard. Their mission: destroy the navy of Queen Elizabeth and open the way for the invasion of England.

The mastermind behind the move, King Phillip II of Spain, angered at the turn of events under Henry VIII which had put Protestants in semi-control of England, set out to reclaim the nation for Roman Catholicism. Moreover, he

## The defeat of the Spanish Armada helped shape the Christian face of North America.

did not like Queen Elizabeth's aid to his rebellious Dutch subjects in Holland who were valiantly fighting the iron hand of Rome.

England came out to meet the Spanish fleet with only seventy ships (over half of them borrowed) and 9,000 men. But she took advantage of the Spanish commander's poor seamanship (he had no naval experience), her own heavier guns and a favorable wind. After a five-day running battle, the English closed in with their fireships on July 28. The Spaniards panicked, cut their cables and fled north in disarray. With half the fleet lost and the crew ravaged by epidemic, the Spanish Armada returned home in dismal defeat.

The event destroyed the pope's last hope of regaining England for Roman Catholicism. Even more far-reaching, it gave England undisputed control of the seas, allowing Protestants to colonize the New World just a few decades later.

Had Spain won this battle and retained her supremacy of the waters, she might well have colonized America. And the Pilgrims and Puritans might never have had the chance to carve out the beginnings of religious liberty and democracy in America.

THE VOYAGE OF THE MAYFLOWER took place more than one hundred twenty years after Columbus had sailed the same Atlantic. The Pilgrims hit shore more than one thousand miles north of where Columbus and his crew had landed. But the trip was no less perilous. And, it seems, the voyage was more frustrating—especially when they tried to do things their own way instead of turning to God.

It had taken months, even years, to finance the trip and finally get underway. One start was aborted when a companion ship, the *Speedwell,* proved unseaworthy and had to turn back. The Separatists from the village of Scrooby, England, together with a delegation of other recruits (called "strangers"), finally set sail by themselves after a temporary stay in Holland.

Halfway across the Atlantic the *Mayflower* and her crew faced near disaster in a terrific storm. "The ship was shrewdly shaken and her upperworks made very leaky; and one of the main beams amidship was bowed and cracked." The band of dissenters and

their guests almost turned back once again. For "even seasoned mariners aboard," say the records, "seemed to fear the sufficiency of the ship."

Christopher Jones, the ship's master, assured all that the vessel was "strong and firm under water and for the buckling of the main beams, there was a great iron screw that the passengers brought out of Holland ... which would raise the beam into his place, which being done, they committed themselves to the will of God and resolved to proceed."

The *Mayflower* plunged on through the seas. But the ocean continued turbulent. The people, crammed into unbelievably tight quarters for such a long journey, grew more and more impatient. Their diary admits "some appearance of faction" aboard with some "not well affected to unity and concord."

The battered ship finally came within sight of Cape Cod on November 19,

1620. But supplies were exhausted. Pilgrim historian Ruth Terhune Huestis describes the plight: "They were utterly without wood for building fires in standboxes aboard to relieve the winter chill, to dry the salt damp out of bedding and to prepare hot gruel or a soup to warm empty stomachs."

The band of pilgrims scanned the shoreline just to the west of them and described it as "a goodly land wooded to the brink of the sea," which was true of Cape Cod at that time. But they had no patent to sanction their going ashore at Cape Cod, for their charter had been issued for the Virginia Colony—still to the south. This was "no man's land." Worse yet, by now there was near anarchy aboard. On ship, Christopher Jones was the law of England. Ashore, he was no more than another Englishman.

At this point, however, "they tacked about and resolved to stand for the southward ... to find some place about

Left: Replica of the Mayflower
Above—A segment of Plymouth Rock

Hudson's River for their habitation."

"Whatever reasoning may have made them turn south southwest, God so disposed that they did not go far. After about half a day they 'fell amongst dangerous shoals and roaring breakers.' Precisely which of the shoal waters or rips threatened the *Mayflower* is unknown, but William Bradford recorded the fact that 'they conceived themselves in great danger' and 'thought themselves happy to get out of those dangers before night overtook them, as by God's providence they did.'"

The ship moved out into deep water again. Her occupants could not go back to the Old World for they were out of provisions. They dared not go forward into the New World, and the seamen were in desperate need of rest. So rest they did, while the shipful of weary immigrants from a far-off continent pondered what to do.

For some unknown reason the *Mayflower* diary was silent about that crisis day of November 20, though it must have been the most critical one in their whole history. But putting the pieces together, historian Huestis draws this conclusion:

"Every man in that ship must have prayed in his heart, for the Lord who sees into men's hearts and invites men to pray in secret rewarded them in that long quiet day. Something happened. The next morning a compact was signed by these lately contentious, opinioned and ambitious men whose good will was deep rooted in love of God and their fellowmen."

That historic agreement was the Mayflower Compact:

Restoration of the Plymouth Colony

In the name of God, Amen. We, whose names are underwritten, the loyal subjects of our dread Sovereign Lord King James, by the grace of God, of Great Britain, France and Ireland; Defender of the Faith & c.

Having undertaken for the glory of God and advancement of the Christian faith and honor of our King and country a Voyage to plant the first Colony in the northern parts of Virginia; do, by these presents, solemnly and mutually, in the presence of God and one of another, covenant and combine our selves together into a civil body politic, for our better ordering and preservation, and furtherance of the ends aforesaid; and by virtue hereof to enact, constitute and frame such just and equal laws, or-dinances, acts, constitutions, offices, from time to time, as shall be thought most meet and convenient for the general good of the Colony, unto which we promise all due submission and obedience.

In witness whereof, we have hereunder subscribed our names...."

Only God could work such a miracle in the hearts of people that they thus, voluntarily, lay aside all thought of self in concern for the welfare of all.

"And that day they 'came to an anchor in the Bay, which is a good harbor ... compassed about to the very sea with pines, juniper, sassafras and other sweet wood.... And there, said Bradford, recounting the event several years later, they 'blessed the God of heaven, who had brought them over the fast and furious ocean ... and a sea of troubles before.... Let them, therefore, praise the Lord, because He is good and His mercies endure forever.' " (Scripture quoted from the *Geneva Bible* used by the Pilgrims.)

The drama of the Mayflower ... the defeat of the Spanish Armada ... the voyage of Columbus, all converge to lay the spiritual and governmental foundations of America.

In one sense, it seems incredible that the vast north American continent lay in complete wilderness as recently as 350 years ago, while across the ocean great civilizations had already risen and fallen more than a thousand years before. Jesus Christ did not come to planet earth until "the fulness of time" (Gal. 4:4). And, so it seems, the rise from the wilderness of an entirely new kind of nation awaited "the fulness of time"—a time when the gospel of the Savior could have free course in her formative years and when that same gospel would help lay the cornerstone of our government and our freedoms.

This could not be by chance, but by design. The founding fathers recognized this, whether or not everyone still does today. John Adams, second president of the United States, once said:

"I always consider the settlement of America with reverence and wonder as the opening of a grand scene and design in Providence for the illumination of the ignorant and the emancipation of the slavish part of mankind all over the world."

## CHAPTER THREE
# THE FOUNDATIONS THEY LAID

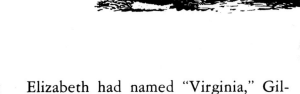

WHEN THE PILGRIMS LANDED at Plymouth Rock in 1620, they carved out of the wilderness the first colony along the northern shoreline of what is now the United States. But this was not the first permanent English settlement in North America. This honor went to Jamestown, Virginia, established thirteen years earlier in 1607, some miles to the south. A vast tract of land known as the Virginia Colony stretched for hundreds of miles along the Atlantic Seaboard, though it was all but uninhabited except for the native Indians.

Sir Humphry Gilbert, half brother of Sir Walter Rawleigh, acquired the first charter to colonize America as far back as 1578, more than four decades before the Pilgrims landed.

But the history of Virginia and Jamestown was one disaster after another.

In 1580, during the second of two attempts to reach the land which Queen Elizabeth had named "Virginia," Gilbert died.

Rawleigh landed a contingent of settlers at Roanoke in 1585 to explore the area for nine months. The Indians lured these adventurers from their main responsibilities by stories of gold and silver mines and rich pearl fisheries. The Englishmen neglected their priorities and soon found themselves in a desperate state of fatigue and famine. Sir Francis Drake discovered their plight on his return from a successful expedition against the Spaniards in the West Indies and carried them home to England.

Shortly after, Rawleigh returned to retrieve his force. But they had vanished. Mystified, Rawleigh left fifteen of his crew to keep possession of the island. The handful of men were soon cut in pieces by the savages.

The next year Captain John White landed three shiploads of settlers once

**Sir Walter Rawleigh
landed a contingent
of settlers at Roanoke in 1585.**

more at Roanoke, and, after looking over the ruggedness of the land with which they would have to contend, he rushed back to England for more supplies. He found the nation in alarm over more important matters—the threat of an invasion from Spain. And so the unfortunate Roanoke colony received no supplies. It too perished.

Finally, on April 26, 1607, one hundred five men landed on the south shore of Chesapeake Bay and established Jamestown, the first permanent English Settlement in North America.

Permanent, yes, in one sense, but destined for calamity.

Almost immediately, animosities broke out among the men. The day after they landed, the men excluded Captain John Smith from their governing council, weakening the colony's leadership. The settlers promptly were in a war with the natives. Their food dwindled and deteriorated. Famine grew. Violence flared. Disease spread. Soon one half of the men had died and most of the others turned sickly.

Captain Smith fortified the Jamestown post. Then with a small detachment he trekked into the forest and secured food from the enemy, either by force or diplomacy. On one such excursion, though, Indians caught him by surprise. Escaping after a gallant defense, he sunk to his neck in a swamp and had to surrender.

Death seemed sure, but the quick-thinking Smith pulled out his mariner's compass and astonished the Indians with its many virtues. The story is legend. The captors led Smith to Chief Powhatan and the place of execution. But at the last moment the favorite daughter of Powhatan rushed in between them and begged her father to spare Smith's life. English writers later dignified her with the title of Princess Pocahontas. Smith was released.

Meanwhile, back at Jamestown, only thirty-eight survived. But "gold fever" soon struck again. King James sent over another contingent of settlers on three ships—one carrying a new charter to keep order in the colony. But the ship with the charter papers went down in a violent hurricane off Bermuda. An accidental explosion of gunpowder then disfigured Smith so badly that he had to return to England. With no strong figure to govern, the wildest anarchy erupted, and only the timely arrival from England of Lord Delaware restored order.

With a new influx of English settlers Jamestown finally began to prosper. Little did they suspect the horror still to come.

Jamestown residents had been supplying firearms to the area Indians, whom they commonly employed as hunters. The English, careless in their security, had spread out into smaller

A Jamestown house restored

Some four decades later Jamestown, still in the backwash of the Indian massacre, battled yet another conflict. England's Navigation Act of 1643, which greatly restricted the Virginia Colony's trade rights, had triggered strife. In addition, an insurgent named Nathaniel Bacon gathered a following of troops and set out to annihilate the Indians. When Governor Berkeley refused him a general's commission, Bacon and his troops suddenly wheeled and marched on the colony capital of Jamestown itself. The conflict that followed reduced settlements along the river.

On the morning of March 22, 1622, they unsuspectingly ushered in several Indian spys sent by Openchancanough, under pretext of delivering presents of venison and fruits. Jamestown had let in the "Trojan horse."

Without warning the Indians attacked and began to massacre. In some settlements not a single Englishman escaped. Survivors, overwhelmed with grief and terror, retreated to safety within the small, original confines of Jamestown and then struck back in revenge. A bloody war ensued.

TWO YEARS BEFORE the Indian massacre, the *Mayflower* Pilgrims had landed at Plymouth Rock. Like the settlers at Jamestown, they too faced great hardship—the winter, disease, hunger. Three months after the landing half were dead, and most of the others sick.

But there was a different spirit among these of the Plymouth Colony.

The few healthy survivors, among them Miles Standish and William Brewster, unselfishly assisted the weak "without any grudging in ye least," wrote William Bradford in his *History of the Plymouth Plantation*.

The colonists established friendly relations with the Indians. Among them was Squanto, who showed the pilgrims how to plant corn.

They gave thanksgiving to God at every evidence of His provision. That first summer the harvest prospered.

But new settlers who would suddenly drift in from the sea without adequate provisions aboard soon strained the

A statue of Pilgrim

food supply. Yet the pilgrims tried to help these folk as best they could.

William Bradford writes of how they rested on God's providence time and time again, "at night not many times knowing wher to have a bitt of any thing ye next day. And so, as one well observed, had need to pray that God would give them their dayly brade, above all people in ye world. Yet they bore these wants with great pateince & allacritie of spirite, and that for so long a time as for ye most parte of 2. years; ..."

Bradford's account also describes a three-month drought. The corn withered, the ground cracked. The settlers set aside "a solemne day of humiliation, to seek ye Lord by humble & fervente prayer, in this great distrese."

The Lord answered.

"For all ye morning, and greatest part of the day, it was clear weather & very hotte, and not a cloud or any signe of raine to be seen, yet toward evening it begane to overcast, and shortly after to raine, with shuch sweete and gentel showers, as gave them cause of rejoyceing, & blesing God.

"It came, without either wind, or

thunder, or any violence, and by degreese in yt abundance, as that ye earth was thorowly wete and soked therewith. Which did so apparently revive & quicken ye decayed corne & other fruits, as was wonderfull to see, and made ye Indeans astonished to behold; and afterwards the Lord sent them shuch seasonable showers, with enterchange of faire warme weather, as, through his blessing caused a fruitfull & liberall harvest, to their no small comforte and rejoycing.

"For which mercie (in time conveniente) they also sett aparte a day of thanksgiveing. This being overslipt in its place, I thought meet here to insert ye same...."

And at an earlier time when the crop prospects had looked sorely inadequate these pilgrims made a strategic decision which later proved of great wisdom.

By arrangement with individual "investors" back in England who had underwritten the pilgrim enterprise, the settlers at first ran a "collective" farming operation.

But when an expected shipment of supplies from England failed to materialize, the situation deteriorated. It was then that the Pilgrims "begane to

**The Pilgrims gave Thanksgiving to God at every evidence of His provision.**

thinke how they might raise as much corne as they could, and obtaine a beter crope then they had done, that they might not still thus languish in miserie."

After much debate they decided that each family should farm its own parcel of land, each operator assuming his own risks and his own potential.

"This had very good success," records Bradford, "for it made all hands very industrious, so as much more corne was planted than other waise wold have bene by any means ye Govr

or any other could use, and saved him a great deall of trouble, and gave farr better contente."

The collective or socialistic approach, observed the pilgrims in retrospect, squelched incentive, bred confusion and discontent and retarded "much imploymet that would have been to their benefite and comforte. For ye yongmen that were most able and fitte for labour & service did repine that they should spend their time & streingth to worke for other mens wives and children, with out any recompence.

"The experience ... may well evince," wrote Bradford, "the vantie of that conceite of Platos & other ancients, applauded by some of later times;—that ye taking away of propertie, and bringing in comunitie into a comone wealth, would make them happy and florishing; as if they were wiser then God."

Settlers at Jamestown had made the

**The Mayflower Compact
helped lay America's foundation
for law and order.**

same discovery—during a period of peace secured by an alliance with Powhatan. They discarded their own brand of communism for private enterprise. Joint labor, the common store house, equal distribution, went out the window. Sir Thomas Dale broke up land into small lots and granted property rights. Production spiraled.

But in their case, success backfired when overzealous planters put most of their land into tobacco, a crop newly introduced with a good market in England, and neglected the staple crops necessary for survival.

Apart from the beginnings of American private enterprise, the Pilgrims at Plymouth, through the *Mayflower Compact,* also laid the foundations of law and order and established the first "Civil Body Politic" in America.

They could not have foreseen, of course, any long-range significance at the time, for it was intended only as a temporary compact to keep law and order among themselves in a wilderness where there was no law.

At the heart of the compact lay an undisputed conviction that God must be at the center of all law and order and that law without a moral base is really no law at all. The compact also rested on a "covenant" agreement, and this was later to help lay the foundations of American democracy. In other words, all laws and obedience to them would rest not upon a monarchy or a dictatorship, but upon "the consent of the governed."

The *Mayflower Compact* served Plymouth well for more than seventy years—until 1691, when the colony united with Massachusetts.

And in brief this is why, today, the inscription on the Plymouth Rock monument along the New England shore reads:

> They laid the foundation
> of a state wherein every man
> through countless ages
> should have liberty.

WHILE THE PILGRIMS carved out their own niche in American history, they were a tiny lot alongside the swarm of Puritans who crossed the ocean and settled along the shores of Massachusetts Bay in the decades that followed.

Like the Pilgrims, Puritans stood at odds with the Church of England and its hierarchy. In their eyes the Reformation had not gone far enough. But, unlike the pilgrims, who were strong separatists, they were not yet ready to "pull out." Instead, they wanted to continue the reformation from within and strive for a "pure" church.

The wild American continent gave them a chance to escape the corruptions they saw in their own church-state homeland, if not to leave the Church of

England itself.

A Puritan minister by the name of John White of Dorchester started the movement to America. He set out to establish a commercial fishing company and, at the same time, to minister to the English fishermen who were beginning to work the New England waters. The company failed, but White promptly saw the opportunity for Christians to establish a colony on new soil where they could model society along biblical lines.

In 1629 England's King Charles granted the Puritans a charter for the Massachusetts Bay Company. Since the goal was religious, and no longer a business venture, why did he allow it? Perhaps the king was more than glad to send some of his sharpest critics far across the ocean! At any rate, again the divine hand of Providence seemed to be molding America.

By little more than a decade later

some 20,000 colonists had made their way across the Atlantic to New England. Many of these were not Puritans. In fact, perhaps less than one fifth even professed to be Christians.

But it was the Puritans who established the government, built the schools, administered the churches and set the moral tone.

The Puritan stood firmly in the tradition of John Calvin, who at one time had established a theocracy in Switzerland. He had no illusions about the nature of man—who was a sinner—and utopian society was a delusion. Law, discipline, control, must prevail. And so the Puritans set up a semi-theocracy or what might be called a "Bible commonwealth." Christians and non-Christians alike lived under a modified church-state rule, which recognized the sovereignty and omniscience of God.

The Puritans argued that it was not a true theocracy. Clerics did not make civil law. Nor did the church hierarchy choose the officers of state (the Puritans themselves had seen enough of this). However, only members of the church could vote in community elections.

Puritan theology rested heavily upon covenant concepts and the Puritans saw themselves essentially as a "people of Israel" in the American wilderness. There was a heavy Old Testament emphasis, though not to the exclusion of the New. Spiritual truth, they insisted, must be taught in all three major arenas of life—the home, the church and the school, and that emphasis remains today among many of the Reformed churches.

The Puritans insisted that conversion precede church membership, and that point was reaffirmed in 1648 with the adoption of the "Cambridge Platform." "The doors of the churches of Christ upon earth," they said, "do not by God's appointment stand so wide open, that all sorts of people good or bad, may freely enter therein at their pleasure." Those seeking admission, they declared, must be "examined and tried first" to see that they possess, above all else, "repentance from sin and faith in Jesus Christ." Potential members usually made "a personal and public confession," detailing "God's manner of working upon the soul."

Years later, however, the Puritans were to relax these requirements with second and third generation offspring who had grown up in the church, many of whom lived good lives but had no conversion experience. This decision, known as the "Half Way Covenant," eventually proved to be the downfall of the Puritans.

In Puritan New England the Bible and education went hand in hand. An unusually high proportion of the early colonists were university graduates.

## 100 Psalm Tune New

Psalm 100, v. 1. from
The Bay Psalm Book

John Tufts.
*An Introduction to the Singing of Psalm Tunes (1726)*

Shout to Je - ho - vah, all ___ the earth. With joy - ful -

Shout to Je - ho - vah, all the earth. With joy - ful -

ness the Lord serve yee. Be - fore his pres - ence

ness the Lord serve yee. Be - fore his pres - ence

come with mirth. Know that Je - ho - vah God __ is hee.

come with mirth. Know that Je - ho - vah God is hee.

How they launched higher education in America is reserved for another chapter. At the core of the elementary program, however, stood the New England Primer and the historic *Bay Psalm Book,* the latter assembled by Richard Mather and John Eliot, two of Puritanism's most illustrious figures.

Essentially the *Bay Psalm Book* contained the Psalms in metre, designed to help children absorb spiritual truth at the same time as they read—and memorized—the Scriptures in poetry form. Psalm 1, for instance, read as follows:

O blessed man, that in the advice
  of wicked doeth not walk:
nor stand in sinners way, nor sit
  in chayre of scornfull folk.
But in the law of Jehovah,
  is his longing delight:
and in his law doth meditate,
  by day and eke by night.
And he shall be like to a tree
  planted by water-rivers:
that in his season yields his fruit,
  and his leafe never withers.
And all he doth, shall prosper well,
  the wicked are not so:
but they are like unto the chaffe,
  which winde drives to and fro.

John Eliot, missionary to the indians, translates the Bible
to Algonquin.

Therefore shall not ungodly men,
   rise to stand in the doome,
nor shall the sinners with the just,
   in their assemblie come.
For of the righteous men, the Lord
   acknowledgeth the way:
but the way of ungodly men,
   shall utterly decay.

THE NAME OF JOHN ELIOT, though,
went in the history books not so
much for his part in the *Bay Psalm Book,*
nor for his more than fifty years as a
pastor in Roxbury. Rather, he became
known for his incredible dedication as a
missionary to the Indians.

John Eliot indeed took to heart the
evangelistic intent behind the Massachusetts Bay charter. He held the
Bible as the literal word of God, the
ultimate source of all knowledge, and
the Indian as a human being who
needed to hear its message. As he
wrote in later years:

"Pity to the poor Indians, and desire
to make the name of Christ chief in
these dark ends of the earth—and not
the rewards of men—were the very first
and chief moves, if I know what did
first and chiefly move in my heart,

when God was pleased to put upon me that work of preaching to them."

The tribes along Massachusetts Bay spoke Algonquian, a Mahican dialect. Eliot began to explore how he might reach them, and before long concluded that he must learn their language.

His key contact proved to be an Indian named Cockenoe, who had been captured in the Pequot War of 1637 and later put to work for a Dorchester planter. Cockenoe could speak and even read English.

With this helper, and later his replacement, Eliot began the tedious task of analyzing this Indian language. The Algonquian had a habit of compressing complex ideas into extended single words. Eliot would surely have earned the esteem of the thousands of Wycliffe Translators today who are at work in similar linguistic missions around the world.

After two years he had translated the Ten Commandments and the Lord's Prayer and could speak Algonquian with hesitation. Cotton Mather declared to Eliot that surely it would be easier to teach the Indians English and then preach the gospel, but Eliot insisted that they should hear the Good News in their native tongue.

That opportunity came on a chilly October day when a peaceful Indian named Waban led Eliot and three companion clergymen into a wigwam along the river a few miles above Cambridge. There at the council fire Eliot preached the first Protestant sermon in the Indian tongue on the North American continent. He took Ezekiel 27:9 as his text. It proved a good choice. The Indians listed intently, some curious, some doubting, a few malicious. Later around their smoldering fires they would ask such questions as:

"Why does not God who has full power kill the Devil that makes all men so bad?"

"Was the Devil or man made first?"

"Why do Englishmen kill all snakes?"

But eventually Waban became a staunch convert to Jesus Christ, and so also did followers. Eliot later gave them clothing, blankets, spades, axes and other tools. He gave the squaws spinning wheels. The Indians laid out streets and fenced and planted their fields. They became known as the "Praying Indians."

But not all the white settlers, on guard as they were, trusted Eliot's "praying Indians," and others wondered if this missionary work was worth the money spent to reach them. As the Indians prospered, Eliot pressed for ten years to translate the entire Bible into Algonquian, sentence by sentence, verse by verse.

"With his other burdens," observes author Francis Russell, "it is a marvel that he found time to carry on his trans-

Cornhusking at Nantucket during Puritan era.

lating. For in all weathers and all seasons he made his visitation in the towns and friendly settlements, sometimes as far as sixty miles afield. An indomitable figure who could bend to a nor'easter and yet not draw back, who did not hesitate a pinch to adopt Indian dress, who would stop on a rainy night at any wigwam and wring the water from his socks and be off the next morning...."

Some of Eliot's Indian converts became teachers and ministers. His work triggered formation of a London corporation called "the Society for Promoting and Propagating the Gospel of Jesus Christ in New England." His "reports from the mission field" eventually became known as the Indian Tracts. Eliot's Algonquian Bible, the *Up-Biblum,* finally came off the Cambridge Press at Harvard in 1663, and two hundred copies bound in stout leather were released for immediate use of the Indians. It was the first Bible printed in America, and the earliest example in history of the translation and printing of the entire Bible as a means of evangelism.

In later years the outbreak of King Philip's War and unfortunate events that followed the conflict destroyed the Indian work, but many remained loyal to the end. They shall be among those of "every tribe, and tongue, and nation"

whom we shall see someday. "He that hath the Son hath life" (I John 5:12). As one writer said of John Eliot himself as he came to the end of a long and dedicated life, "For him the Great Perhaps was a certainty."

PURITAN NEW ENGLAND strongly helped shape the foundations of the nation to come. Men like John Cotton and Increase Mather preached forcefully from her pulpits along with many lesser known. But the influx of new settlers each year, along with other forces, gradually eroded the foundations of the Bible commonwealth. And there arose other voices—even the voices of dedicated, evangelical Christians—who thought that such a commonwealth ought not be imposed on the entire populace. In fact, they saw the commonwealth as a threat both to good government and to good Christianity. Let there be, they said, a separation of church and state.

One of those voices belonged to Roger Williams. Like the pilgrims, Williams was a separatist Christian. But as a youth he had established influential friendships with the Puritans, which stood him in good stead in later years when he sought charter for his colony of Rhode Island.

Williams challenged head-on the

basis of the Massachusetts Bay government. He argued for a compact theory of government that rested entirely on "the consent of the governed." He contended that good civil government and also a vigorous Christian faith could indeed flourish in a land that allowed religious liberty for all.

When magistrates threatened to export him from the colony for such views, Williams plunged into the forest and wandered for fourteen weeks. He eventually found hospitality among the Indians. In time he purchased from them some land on the Mohassuck and founded the town of Providence. Other followers settled what is now Portsmouth and Newport, and a third group took abode on the west side of Narragansett Bay. The Rhode Island colony promised its people "peaceful and quiet enjoyment of lawful right and liberty," ...not withstanding our different consciences touching the truth as it is in Jesus."

Williams and others likeminded also took issue with the practice of infant baptism and it was in Rhode Island that the first Baptist churches began to emerge. Soon they also appeared in the older Puritan colonies.

Despite their sharp differences in viewpoint, there is evidence that Williams and Massachusetts Governor Winthrop maintained a genuine Christian friendship in their later years. By 1687 Williams saw a new Massachusetts charter sweep away the Puritan requirement that permitted only church members to vote.

What the early Puritans gave American culture, says one observer, amounts to much more than the "blue laws," the witch-trials (a bleak episode for which those involved later repented) and the stern religious doctrine for which they are sometimes known.

The Puritans gave us free public education, a thoroughgoing respect for learning, our first books, our first college (see chapter five) and the habit of representative government.

"That they had time for intellectual concerns," writes this analyst, "is remarkable. They were faced not only with the formidable tasks of conquering the wilderness and setting up trade, but with providing for such physical necessities as food, clothing and shelter. Yet they did not lose sight of the value of the printed page. As early as 1640 a printing press was turning our books. Taxes were levied for public education."

THE RELIGIOUS LIBERTY for which Roger Williams and others opted became reality as settlers pushed inland. New colonies emerged—like Pennsylvania, New Jersey, Delaware.

In this movement, William Penn stands out as a giant for his influence and vision in the arena of religious freedom.

William Penn's treaty with the indians in 1681 when he founded Pennsylvania.

In England in 1670 William Penn had just received a very large inheritance from his father, who, incidentally, discovered the island of Bermuda. In addition, he was due a settlement of a debt of 16,000 pounds due the estate of his father from the Crown.

For this settlement Penn conceived the idea of obtaining a grant of land in America. He petitioned the king for a tract of land "lying north of Maryland, on the east bounded with Delaware River, on the West limited as Maryland is, and northward to extend as far as plantable, which is altogether Indian."

The venture might at first sound like the spoiled son out to spend his father's wealth on a wild speculative scheme. But note the young man's driving motive as he writes to a friend:

"Because I have been somewhat exercised at times about the nature and end of government among men, it is reasonable to expect that I should endeavor to establish a just and righteous one in this province, that others may take example by it,—truly this my heart desires. For the nations want a precedent.... I do, therefore, desire the Lord's wisdom to guide me, and those that may be concerned with me, that we do the thing that is truly wise and just.

"And again,—'For my country, I eyed the Lord in obtaining it, and more was I drawn inward to look to Him, and to owe it to His hand and power than to any other way. I have so obtained it, and desire to keep it that I may not be unworthy of His love....'"

William Penn, who had become a Quaker, deplored bias and had a keen social conscience. To him the king gave what later became one of the largest states in the northeast U.S., with right to govern. A year later the Duke of York gave to Penn what is now Delaware.

A lesser man might have squandered this large piece of real estate, to the detriment of generations to come, if not the nation itself. But not Penn. He perceived that the God who had "given it me through many difficulties, will, I believe, bless and make it the seed of a nation..."

Into this territory of liberty later poured the sons and daughters of many nations—the Dutch, the Swedes, the Welsh, English Quakers, several German groups and, last, the Scotch-Irish.

Not a few of these settlers abused their liberties. At one point Penn observed that "liberty without obedience is confusion, and obedience without liberty is slavery." But Penn's "Holy Experiment," despite some disappointments to him personally, survived to become a major cornerstone in the foundation of America.

IF THE DRAMA behind the making of America says anything at this point, surely it shouts out the sovereign hand of God and declares that a minority of dedicated Christians can make an impact on society far beyond their numbers. The pilgrims were a minority. The Puritans, though many, were still in the minority. Roger Williams and William Penn stood with the minority. Though many of the early settlers were Christians, far more were not. Yet what great impact these Christians made, and what foundations they laid.

"For other foundation can no man lay than that which is laid, which is Jesus Christ" (1 Cor. 3:11).

Penn also set an example of sympathetic treatment toward the American Indians, unfortunately not true of some colonists. James Hefley in his booklet, *America: One Nation Under God*, points out that Penn "insisted that settlers in his colony purchase land from the Indians for a fair price. He abolished imprisonment for debt and also insisted that in court cases involving Indians, at least half of the jury must be red men."

Jonathan Edward set a similar example when he asked the members of his congregation to sign a covenant pledging, among other things, to refrain from defrauding their neighbors whether Indian or European, cheating them out of debts, or "breaching moral equity" in any commercial transaction. And David Brainerd was appalled to find white men using alcohol to cheat Indians of their lands. "The revival that resulted from his preaching of the gospel," observes Hefley, "stopped much of the injustice. Dishonest traders tried in vain to discredit Brainerd by spreading stories that he intended to trap the Indians and sell them to the British as slaves."

CHAPTER FOUR

# THROUGH A REVOLUTION

ON A CRISP NIGHT in December, 1774, three shiploads of tea from England drifted restlessly at their moorings in Boston Harbor. The colonists liked their tea, but they were not about to let these merchants of the British East-India Company unload their cargo. England had just imposed a three-cents-a-pound duty, and Americans saw this scheme as both a monopoly and "taxation without representation."

But the tension had been building for a long time. It began after the French and Indian War, when England barred her growing colonies from settling lands beyond the Allegheny Mountains. And when Britain levied taxes on her colonies but failed to seat their representatives in Parliament. And when the Americans were forced to "quarter" English troops in their homes, and when men like Franklin, Jefferson and Adams became convinced that Britain had usurped many of the colonists' rights.

Tea-laden ships from the same English convoy had also put in at the ports of New York, Philadelphia and Charleston. They too were refused permission to unload.

This firm stance triggered exultation throughout the colonies and united the American patriots behind the cause of liberty as had no event to that hour.

If any one man's influence triggered the Boston Tea Party, it would have to be that of Samuel Adams. History labels him the "Father of the American Revolution."

ADAMS WAS NOT simply a rabble-rouser, nor an irresponsible revolutionist intent on tearing down the system. Thomas Jefferson once said of him that "his feet were ever in the stirrup, his lance ever in its rest."

But Samuel Adams had been telling

**Samuel Adams saw individual freedom as "the law of the Creator" and a Christian right documented in the New Testament.**

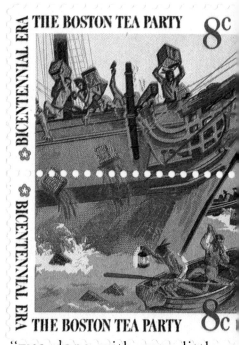

THE BOSTON TEA PARTY

his countrymen for years that America had to take her stand against tyranny. He regarded individual freedom as "the law of the Creator" and a Christian right documented in the New Testament.

And he insisted that his fellow colonists should reason out these inherent Christian rights in the free marketplace where people could discuss, dispute, debate. And so over the years prior to the Revolution he took a vigorous role in the Boston Town Meeting, and encouraged his fellowmen to do likewise. He also established "committees of correspondence" to spread by letter the ideas of liberty throughout the colonies. But he stressed "constitutional principles," rather than "issues," so that people might ultimately act through lawful means, not by riot and rebellion.

What then of the Boston Tea Party, which Adams and thousands of others applauded? To some today it comes off as an act of violence akin to those perpetrated by modern day revolutionists—and not a few have exploited this historical event to justify their anarchy.

But the Boston Tea Party was nothing of the kind. No one was injured; no one harmed. The protestors destroyed no property but the tea itself, which the colonists later offered to pay for.

Nor did the crowds watching from shore seize the occasion to vandalize the town. "The whole," Hutchinson wrote, "was done with very little tumult." The town was never more still of a Saturday night than it was at ten o'clock that evening.

**B**UT MEN FROM BOSTON carried the news to other villages throughout the colonies: Boston had stood her ground against the growing British threat to liberty.

Among those on guard at the Boston harbor that eventful night was John Hancock, a close compatriot of Adams. Both men were later to put their signatures on the Declaration of Independence. Hancock stood by with others watching the tea spill into the waters—and rejoiced!

It was Hancock and Adams whom the British promptly labeled as their two most wanted men. On the night of Paul Revere's famous midnight ride, they were sleeping at the home of Rev. Jonas Clark in Lexington. Revere arrived about midnight, having narrowly escaped British capture earlier in the evening, to find a guard of eight men stationed on the premises for the protection of Hancock and Adams.

He requested admittance but the Sergeant replied that the family had retired and asked that they might not be disturbed by any noise about the house.

"Noise!" replied Revere, "You'll have noise enough before long. The Regulars are coming out!"

He got in.

At daybreak the guard ushered Adams and Hancock off to a nearby village, their safety regarded as being of utmost importance. As they passed through the fields while the sunlight glistened in the dew of the fresh morning, Adams sensed the dawn of a nation and exclaimed, "O! what a glorious morning is this!"

Later in Independence Hall, only hours before the signing of the Declaration of Independence, he would remark to Benjamin Rush: "If it were revealed to me that nine hundred Americans out of every thousand will perish in a war for liberty, I would vote for that war rather than see my country enslaved. The survivors of such a war, though few, would propagate a nation of free men."

The same morning that Hancock and Adams made their escape, a militia of minutemen and the British confronted each other on the nearby Lexington village green. There suddenly erupted a deadly volley of fire (no one is absolutely sure who fired first). It was a "shot heard 'round the world."

The inevitable War of Revolution against the hand of tyranny had begun. After the battles of Lexington and Concord, the British retreated to nearby Boston where, at high cost, they dislodged the colonial militia in the Battle of Bunker Hill. Colonial troops also suffered defeat in the Quebec Campaign. But despite these initial blows, the flame of the revolution could not be snuffed out, and a momentus act of independence lay just around the corner.

THE DECLARATION OF INDEPENdence went out over such famous names as Franklin, Jefferson, Hancock, John and Samuel Adams. Among the fifty-odd legislators who gathered to debate this revolutionary document of freedom was just one clergyman—John Witherspoon.

Only a few short years before, the gifted preacher and educator had been called over from Scotland to head up the College of New Jersey (now Princeton). He was a strong family man with a deep prayer life (which included a day set apart with his housefold the last day of every year for fasting, humiliation and prayer).

Franklin, Jefferson and Adams, leaders in the struggle for liberty

As war shadows thickened in the American Colonies, Congress had seen the seriousness of the situation and designated May 17, 1776, as a day of national fasting and prayer. They asked John Witherspoon to deliver the sermon. And so he did—speaking solemnly on "The Dominion of Providence over the Affairs of Men." He based his views squarely on Scripture and spoke of God's eternal purpose as unfolded in the drama of historical development—and delineated the issues of liberty as he saw them.

In a short time Witherspoon had gained such respect, both as a college president and keen political observer, that New Jersey elected him delegate to the 1776 Continental Congress.

Witherspoon felt strongly that ministers of the gospel should not become entangled in civil affairs. "When our blessed Saviour says, 'My kingdom is not of this world,'" he once preached, "he plainly intimates to his disciples that they have no title to intermeddle with state affairs."

But as a Christian citizen, Witherspoon accepted the challenge.

War clouds hung heavily over the colonies on July 1, 1776, and rain clouds dropped a downpour on the Philadelphia meeting site. Promptly at 9 o'clock John Hancock called the Congress to order. But Witherspoon—along with the four other New Jersey delegates—did not show.

**As war clouds thickened,
Congress designated May 17, 1776,
as a day of national fasting and prayer.**

By afternoon the question whether or not to declare independence at this hour stood in doubt. Those against it had marshalled their arguments, and a prodeclaration by John Adams, not known for his strong oratory anyway, still left the outcome in doubt.

At that moment the door opened to admit the delegation from New Jersey.

"We are sorry to be late," said Witherspoon. "We have been held up by the storm."

They shed their wet greatcoats and formally enrolled.

"May we ask for a review of the arguments," Witherspoon said.

No answer.

He repeated his request.

"You already know the arguments," John Adams said.

"That is true but we have not heard them *in Congress*."

Adams began to review the case. As he did so, he sensed the New Jersey delegation's impatience for independence. Their moral support seemed to give Adams new life. He ended in a burst of eloquence.

Witherspoon jumped to his feet and called out, "New Jersey is plump for independence."

"The oratory is fine but the facts show we're not ripe for it," said John Alsop of New York.

Granite-faced John Witherspoon fixed his flashing eyes on Alsop and thundered, "We are more than ripe for it, and some of us are in danger of rotting for want of it!"

"Hear, hear!" roared Samuel Adams.

"Hear, hear!" rang out from all sections of the room.

Someone called for a trial vote.

Nine delegations voted for adoption of the Declaration, two against, one undecided, one abstained.

But final action would wait another three days. Meanwhile, the Congress feverishly worked over the proposed articles of Confederation and took time to hear reports from the battlefield.

ON JULY 4 the document was ready for final vote. But a few of the most cautious delegates still won-

Concord Bridge: Symbol of early American resistance.

dered—not about independence itself, but about the timing.

John Witherspoon put their fears to rest:

"There is a tide in the affairs of men," he said. "We perceive it now before us. To hesitate is to consent to our own slavery. That noble instrument should be subscribed to this very morning by every pen in this house. Though these gray hairs must soon descend to the sepulchre, I would infinitely rather that they descend thither by the hand of the executioner than desert at this crisis the sacred cause of my country."

No one spoke.

John Hancock ordered a reading of the final draft:

"When, in the course of human events, it becomes necessary for one people to dissolve the political bands which have connected them with another, and to assume, among the powers of the earth, the separate and equal station to which the laws of nature and of nature's God entitle them, a decent respect to the opinions of mankind, requires that they should declare the causes which impel them to the separation.

"We hold these truths to be self-evident: that all men are created equal, that; they are endowed by their Creator with certain inalienable rights; that among these are life, liberty, and the pursuit of happiness. That to secure

The Minuteman: Symbol of American readiness to defend freedom and liberty

**A reverent hush fell over the hall.
Some looked out the window.
Some prayed.**

these rights, governments are instituted among men, deriving their just powers from the consent of the governed; that whenever any form of government becomes destructive of these ends, it is the right of the people to alter or abolish it, and to institute a new government, laying its foundation on such principles, and organizing its powers in such form, as to them shall seem most likely to effect their safety and happiness...."

SECRETARY CHARLES THOMSON called for the vote, starting with the New England colonies and moving south. One "aye" followed another. It was unanimous.

A reverent hush fell over the hall. Some looked out the window. Some prayed.

The Secretary placed the document on the Speaker's table and looked at the President of Congress. He fingered his goose-quill pen. Then with a flourish and bold strokes John Hancock put his signature on one of the greatest papers of all time.

"There," he said with a smile. "His Majesty can now read my name without glasses. And he can also double the price on my head."

The final signed draft was sent to the printer and, contrary to tradition, it was not signed by others until August 2. Among those who signed at that time was John Witherspoon, who by God's providence had found himself in the right place at the right time.

The public announcement came July 8. Outside in the streets of Philadelphia people gathered in clusters to hear the decision.

In the steeple of the old State House hung a bell on which, by a happy coincidence, was inscribed, these words of Scripture: "Proclaim liberty throughout all the land unto all the inhabitants thereof."

That morning the bellringer went to his post, having placed his boy below to await the announcement, that his bell might be the first to peal forth the glad tidings.

He waited long. Impatiently the old man shook his head and repeated, "They will never do it!"

Suddenly he heard his boy clapping his hands and shouting, "Ring! Ring!"

Grasping the iron tongue, he swung it to and fro, proclaiming the glad news of liberty to all the land.

The crowded streets caught up the sound. Every steeple re-echoed it.

All that night, by shouts, and illuminations, and booming of cannon, the people declared their joy.

AMERICANS HAD SECURED their independence, but another five years of war lay ahead. The battle ground of the Revolution shifted to

New York, where two British brothers, General William Howe and Admiral Richard Howe, overpowered Washington's under-equipped forces in three successive engagements. Washington retreated to New Jersey, but, by the winter of 1776, he mustered his meager army to cross the ice-covered Delaware and launch a surprise attack on the enemy at Trenton and Princeton. The colonialists then soundly defeated General John Burgoyne's British forces in the Battle of Saratoga in 1777.

But Washington's forces could not stop Howe's advance on Philadelphia, and his army was forced to endure the terrible winter at Valley Forge. Half starved and frozen, they wrestled the elements while the British sat smugly in Philadelphia growing fat on American bread and beef, their barracks warmed by American firewood. As his troops cried for meat and other needs,

Washington was helpless, and a letter to the Governor of New Jersey reflected near despair.

American legend says that on this occasion George Washington got on his knees somewhere in those cold woods and prayed. "No letter or diary survives to give eyewitness testimony," wrote Thomas Fleming in *Reader's Digest* (Washington's Prayer at Valley Forge, Feb. '74), but "legends usually incorporate an element of truth." And it would have been entirely within Washington's character to do this, says Fleming, citing a letter the general penned to his favorite chaplain, Rev. Israel Evans, as his Army was emerging from the worst of Valley Forge's travail. Wrote the Revolutionary Commander:

"It will ever be the first wish of my heart to aid your pious endeavours to inculcate a due sense of the dependence we ought to place in that all wise and powerful Being on whom alone our success depends."

Concludes Fleming in the *Reader's*

The old North Church, Boston

*Digest* report: "There is no doubt that in the greatness of Washington's character, which looms larger in history than any legend about him, there was a profound sense of humility before that Being whom he called "the all-powerful guide and great disposer of human events."

The nightmare of Valley Forge slowly but surely shifted back toward the American dream. The French helped turn the tide. At Valley Forge, the Marquis de Lafayette and Baron von Steuben helped shape the despair-ing patriots into a powerful striking force. Succumbing to the diplomacy of Benjamin Franklin, France (who later also gave us our Statue of Liberty) agreed to send troops, ships and money. The British, fearful of being cut off by the French navy, retreated to New York, and Washington moved his forces to West Point.

While encamped here on the Hudson River in 1780, the treachery of Benedict Arnold almost—but not quite—brought disaster. The plot was exposed at the very last minute.

MEANWHILE, on the western frontier, the daring warfare of George Rogers Clark bolstered colonial spirits, and on the seas John Paul Jones subdued the British ship, *Serapis*. The war then shifted to the South—where the prospects at first appeared bleak. Savannah had fallen in 1778, Charleston in 1780. But troops under Nathaniel Greene finally pushed the British north to Yorktown.

Colonial troops under Lafayette held the British long enough to allow a combined American and French force to march down from New York. They arrived just as Admiral de Grasse brought the French fleet into Chesapeake Bay. British General Cornwallis saw he was

Washington Crossing the Delaware

## Was it not of God
## that both the navy and army should enter
## the Chesapeake at the same time?

The Liberty Bell
and Leviticus 25:10

both outnumbered and encircled. He surrendered at Yorktown on October 19, 1781, and the American Revolution was over.

Two years later the British recognized the sovereignty and power of the new nation in the Treaty of Paris.

At many points the Revolutionary War might have been lost. Ezra Stiles, president of Yale, in a major address before the Assembly of Connecticut in 1783, reviewed these events and suggested why near disasters time and time again suddenly turned to victories:

"In our lowest and most dangerous estate, in 1776 and 1777, we sustained ourselves against the British army of sixty thousand troops, commanded by ... the ablest generals Britain could pro-

cure throughout Europe, with a naval force of twenty-two thousand seamen in above eighty British men-of-war ... Who but a Washington, inspired by Heaven, could have struck out the great movement and manoeuvre at Princeton?

"To whom but the Ruler of the winds shall we ascribe it that the British reinforcement, in the summer of 1777, was delayed on the ocean three months by contrary winds, until it was too late for the conflagrating General Clinton to raise the siege of Saratoga?

"What but a providential miracle detected the conspiracy of Arnold, even in the critical moment of the execution of that infernal plot, in which the body of the American army, then at West Point, with his Excellency General Washington himself, were to have been rendered into the hands of the enemy? Was it not of God that both the navy and army should enter the Chesapeake at the same time?

"On the French role in the Revolution he added, "It is God who so ordered the balancing interests of nations as to produce an irresistible motive in the European maritime powers to take our part ..."

In that same Hartford address the Yale president called for "a tranquil period for the unmolested Accomplishment of the *Magnalia Dei*—the great events in God's moral gov-

Bell Tower, Independence Hall—Philadelphia

ernment designed from eternal ages to be displayed in these ends of the earth..."

THEN THE PRESIDENT OF YALE seemed to view the future with remarkable clarity, as if looking directly into the Twentieth Century.

"We shall have a communication with all nations in commerce, manners, and science, beyond anything heretofore known in the world ...

"... The English language ... will probably become the vernacular tongue of more numerous millions than ever yet spake one language on earth" (to which Stiles attributed Christian missionary significance).

"Navigation will carry the American flag around the globe itself ..."

From the Scriptures he seemed to foresee something of today's modern high-speed travel between continents and the world's explosion of technolo-

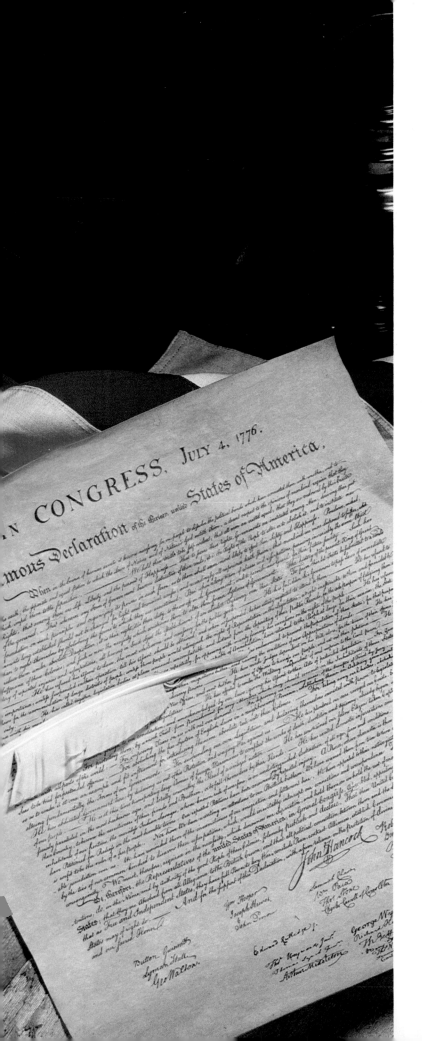

gy. Declared Stiles: "That prophecy of Daniel is now literally fulfilling—'there shall be a universal travelling to and fro, and knowledge shall be increased' (See Dan. 12:4).

"This knowledge will be brought home and treasured up in America, and being here digested and carried to the highest perfection, may reblaze back from America to Europe, Asia, and Africa, and illumine the world with truth and liberty...."

But even back then Stiles warned that the entire American system, good as it was, would prosper only insofar as "men, not merely nominally Christians (Christians in name only), made it work. In view of God's hand in the astonishing events of the Revolution, he concluded, "The United States are under peculiar obligations to become a holy people unto the Lord our God."

Who can miss the hand of God in U.S. history?

Even events centuries before stand out in the divine scenario.

If France had not stopped the Mohammedans at the Battle of Tours, Islam would have conquered Europe and snuffed out any hope of a Christian nation across the seas in the centuries to come.

We have already cited the significance of Columbus' voyage—one that brought back the news of discovery. Yet the winds and other incidents took him

**In a quirk of history,
no man got caught in such a strange
conflict of loyalties as did Jacob Duche.**

irresistably far enough southwest that it saved the Eastern seaboard from early Spanish control. Later the defeat of the Spanish Armada cleared the route once and for all.

Yet the land remained almost untouched until the Reformation had taken firm root.

But startling as it may seem to some today, both the French and the Spanish at one time controlled two thirds of the United States!

Spain set up the first government in the West in Santa Fe (New Mexico) eleven years before the Pilgrims stumbled on Cape Cod. Moreover, the French started their colonial experiment in North America (in what is now Canada) a hundred years before the *Mayflower.*

Yet Spain faded from the U.S. real estate scene, first in Florida, then from the vast West. And then, in the great Louisiana Purchase, the French, under Napoleon, sold almost the entire Midwest to the United States for a bargain price.

THE AMERICAN REVOLUTION ushered in a "land of liberty," but not without its price. And as in any crisis so complex, many faced agonizing decisions. Anglicans, in particular, had a dilemma: should they remain loyal to the motherland of their church and its episcopacy, or fight for the freedoms of the revolution?

The widespread concern that the Church of England would eventually "land a Bishop" on American soil played no small part in cultivating the soil of the revolution. For many feared that with such an event would surely come another church-state, ruled by the English Parliment, with the loss of whatever freedoms already achieved.

In a quirk of history, perhaps no man got caught in such a strange conflict of loyalties as did an Episcopal clergyman of Philadelphia named Jacob Duche.

The First Continental Congress, held about seven months before the outbreak of war, was in session in Philadelphia. But is seemed to be getting nowhere. Religious diversity and other differences threatened the search for national unity. John Adams of Massachusetts detected a fear among Southerners, predominantly Episcopalian, that the Congregationalists of New England wished to rule the continent. So he proposed that they invite in a clergyman to lead them in prayer. Some objected—on grounds that it would be too hard to find one suitable to all.

Adams then suggested Duche, a gesture of tolerance which immediately reassured others that the New England delegates were not insisting on domination.

Duche came the next day and read Psalm 35, appointing it the liturgy for

Inside Carpenters Hall, Philadelphia.

the day.

"Plead thou my cause, O Lord, with them that fight against me ... avenge now my cause, my God and my Lord."

Then he prayed: "Defeat the malicious designs of our cruel adversaries ... Be Thou present, O Lord of wisdom, and direct the council of the honorable assembly...." The entire Psalm fit the occasion beautifully. By the time Duche had finished, many of the delegates were weeping. John Adams was prompted to "confess I never heard a better prayer or one so well-pronounced." He said he "never saw a greater effect upon an audience."

Three years later during the winter of 1777-78 the British captured Philadelphia. Duche wavered momentarily between his loyalty to America and his loyalty to the king who was head of his Church. Then, as a self-admitted Tory, he fled for England and left behind the nation whose first Congress he had so united and inspired!

A S THE HEAVY HAND of political oppression weighed down on the colonists, much of the exhortation for liberty came from the pulpits of the land.

The repeal of the British-imposed Stamp Act, which colonists so utterly resented, prompted Jonathan Mayhew in 1766 to preach a thanksgiving discourse:

"Having ... learned from the holy scriptures that wise, brave, and virtuous men were always friends to liberty; that God gave the Israelites a king (or absolute monarch) in his anger, because they had not sense and virtue enough to be like a free commonwealth and to have himself for their king; that the Son of God came down from heaven to make us 'free indeed'; and that where the Spirit of the Lord is, there is liberty;—this made me conclude that freedom was a great blessing."

The majority of the people at large had little regard for priests, councils or creeds. Congregationalists and Baptists ran simple, democratic church organizations; Presbyterians had chosen a republican form. The fact was, American Protestants were far in advance of their counterparts abroad in religious liberty,

**Well before the American Revolution itself, Christians had laid the foundations for political liberty.**

and so well before the American Revolution itself Christians had laid the foundations for political liberty.

By the time of the Revolution the arguments for freedom had weakened even loyal Anglican ties. Years before the Revolution, for instance, Presbyterian Samuel Davies had espoused the cause of religious liberty and civil independence among the Anglican establishment of the southern colonies. It was in St. John's Episcopal Church, Richmond, Virginia, that Patrick Henry called for both liberty of body and soul when he cried, "Give me liberty or give me death!"

And it was an Anglican, Charles Pinckney, who determined the Constitutional safeguard concerning religion when he proposed the clause in Article VI that "no religious test shall ever be required as a qualification to any office or public trust under the United States." Two thirds of the signers of the Declaration of Independence were members of the Established Church.

Baptists, though not yet great in number at the time of the Revolutionary War, greatly advanced the cause of religious and political liberty, especially in Virginia. Methodism's John Wesley, however, took the Tory side. Promptly all of his English ministers were shipped back to England—except Francis Asbury, who determined to identify himself with the Americans. The major-

ity of native Methodist preachers, however, were loyal to the cause of liberty—and the Methodist revival reached its high point in Virginia at the opening of the Revolution. By the end of the war Methodists had tripled their membership.

The Congregationalists gave overwhelming support to the War for Independence, as did also the Presbyterians and the Baptists. One New England minister, says church historian William Warren Sweet, upon hearing the news from Lexington, preached a farewell sermon, then called his people to arms and marched away with twenty men, recruiting others as they went.

James Caldwell, a pastor and chaplain of a New Jersey regiment, came to the rescue of patriots when wadding for their muskets ran low during a skirmish. He ran to a nearby Presbyterian Church and came back with an armful of Isaac Watts' Psalm Books yelling, "Now, boys, give them Watts!"

The incident inspired poet Bret Harte to write:
> ... They were left in the lurch
> For the want of more wadding, he ran to the church,
> Broke the door, stripped the pews, and dashed out in the road
> With his arms full of hymn-books, and threw down his load
> At their feet. Then above all the shouting and shots
> Rang his voice: "Put Watts into 'em! Boys, give 'em Watts."

## CHAPTER FIVE

# HOW EVANGELICALS LAUNCHED THE IVY LEAGUE

HARVARD, YALE, PRINCETON, DARTMOUTH—These famous universities are part of New England's Ivy League. Probably no other segment of American higher education has turned out a greater number of illustrious graduates—right from the start. And to many even today these prestigious schools represent the elite secular universities in the U.S.

Yet most Americans do not realize that, with the exception of Cornell University in New York and the University of Pennsylvania, every Ivy League school was established primarily to train ministers of the gospel and to evangelize the eastern seaboard.

*Harvard*, 1638: It took only eighteen years from the time the pilgrims set foot on Plymouth Rock until the Puritans, who were among the most educated peoples of their day, founded the first and perhaps most famous Ivy League school. Their story, in brief, is etched today above the gates of Harvard:

"After God had carried us safe to New England, and we had built our houses, provided necessaries for our livelihood, reared convenient places for God's worship, and settled the civil government; one of the next things we longed for, and looked after was to advance learning, and perpetuate it to posterity; dreading to leave an illiterate ministry to the churches, when our present ministers shall lie in the dust."

Harvard College's first presidents and tutors insisted that there could be no true knowledge or wisdom without Jesus Christ, and but for their passionate Christian convictions, there would have been no Harvard.

Harvard's "Rules and Precepts" adopted in 1646 included the following essentials:

"Every one shall consider the main end of his life and studies to know God

and Jesus Christ which is eternal life.

"Seeing the Lord giveth wisdom, every one shall seriously by prayer in secret seek wisdom of him.

"Every one shall so exercise himself in reading the Scriptures twice a day that they be ready to give an account of their proficiency therein, both in theoretical observations of languages and logic, and in practical and spiritual truths ..."

This Christian purpose and campus atmosphere accounts for the fact that, according to reliable calculation, fifty-two percent of the seventeenth-century Harvard graduates became ministers!

*Yale*, 1701: By the turn of the century Christians in the Connecticut region launched Yale as an alternative to Harvard. Many thought Harvard too far away and too expensive, and they also observed that the spiritual climate at Harvard was not what it once had been.

*Princeton*, 1746: This school, originally called "The College of New Jersey," sprang up in part from the impact of the First Great Awakening, a story in itself later in this chapter. It also retained its evangelical vigor longer than any of the other Ivy League schools.

*Dartmouth*, 1754: A strong missionary thrust launched this school in New Hampshire. Its royal charter, signed by King George III of England, specified the school's intent to reach the Indian tribes, and to educate and Christianize English youth as well. Eleazar Wheelock, a close friend of evangelist George Whitefield, secured the charter. In his own home he had already educated a Mohican youth, Samson Occum, who became a distinguished Indian preacher and the author of the hymn 'Awakened by Sinai's Awful Sound.'

Encouraged by his success with Occum, Wheelock envisioned a school that would train Indians to reach their own people. A farmer named John Moor contributed a house and two acres of land, and so the institution

**Harvard's first presidents and tutors insisted there could be no true knowledge or wisdom without Jesus Christ.**

started out as "Moor's Charity School." Later it became Dartmouth.

With the exception of the University of Pennsylvania, every collegiate institution founded in the colonies prior to the Revolutionary War was established by some branch of the Christian church. Even at Penn, however, an evangelist played a prominent part. When Philadelphia churches denied George Whitefield access to their pulpits, forcing him to preach in the open, some of Whitefield's admirers, among them Benjamin Franklin, decided to erect a building to accommodate the great crowds that wanted to hear him. The structure they built became the first building of what is now the University of Pennsylvania, and a statue of Whitefield stands prominently on that campus today.

The first president of New York's Columbia University, first known as "King's College," was an outstanding Christian man named Dr. Samuel

Johnson, who at one time served as a missionary to America under the English-based "Society for the Propagation of the Gospel in Foreign Parts."

Brown University originated with the Baptist churches scattered along the Atlantic seaboard. They established the college to train ministers for the several church groups who, even at that time, strongly believed in separation of church and state.

Cornell University stands as the only Ivy League school whose origins have no particular connection to evangelical Christians. But this is no surprise, since it did not come along until 1865, well after secular trends had become established in the nation's college system.

From the outset the Puritans had put a stress on education. Only five years after they established the Massachusetts Bay Colony the Puritans launched in Boston the first elementary school supported directly by public taxes. But in 1647 they passed an ordinance of far greater significance in the history of our country because it marked the beginning of the American public school system. This ordinance virtually lies at the foundation of all subsequent school legislation and has rightly been termed "the mother of our school laws."

The ordinance, among other things, required at least one qualified school-teacher for every fifty householders,

and a grammar school in every town of more than one hundred families. It also put the Bible in the center of its curriculum, asserting that it is "one chief project of that old deluder, Satan, to keep men from the knowledge of the Scriptures ..."

In most public schools today the Bible is conspicuous by its absence. Obviously, it also is no longer at the center of study in today's universities, such as those in the Ivy League.

What happened along the way? How did Christians eventually "lose" the Ivy League? A brief analysis might teach us something about how to keep today's Christian schools from eventually drifting into the same kind of spiritual disaster.

Statue of George Whitefield on the University of Penn Campus

LOOK FIRST AT HARVARD. Although the founders were strict Puritans, they claimed to permit freedom in matters of theology and made no religious requirement of college officers. And so Harvard was swept away from its evangelical foundations almost completely during the great Unitarian wave that splashed through eastern Massachusetts at the end of the 1700's.

Some tried to head off the Unitarian invaders in a last-minute stand "at the pass," but it proved too late. Among those orthodox defenders of the faith who spoke up the loudest was the Rev. Jedidiah Morse, whose son Samuel invented the Morse code.

From the start Yale, in its Christian stance, had been more conservative than Harvard—perhaps in part because Yale's founders could see even at that time the apostasy of Harvard. But eventually it too drifted, partly in concern for academic excellence amidst an environment of Unitarianism and agnosticism. Also, it took a rather cool stance toward some of the more emotional elements of the First Great Awakening.

The religious atmosphere of Yale improved with the election of Timothy Dwight as president in 1795. He met the students on their own ground and in a series of frank discussions both in the classroom and in the college chapel he treated such subjects as "The Nature and Danger of Infidel Philosophy" and "Is the Bible the Word of God?" He also preached a notable series of sermons in the college chapel on "Theology Explained and Defended," in which he grappled with the principles of deism and materialism. As a result, a revival began in which a third of the student body professed conversion.

In your hymnal you will find Timothy Dwight the author of such works as *I Love Thy Kingdom, Lord* ...

> I love Thy Kingdom, Lord,
> The house of Thine abode,
> The Church our blest Redeemer
>     saved
> With His own precious blood.

In 1828 the "Illinois Band," composed of fourteen dedicated Yale theological students, went forth to evangelize Illinois. This group influenced other similar movements throughout the territory and helped to make Yale an influential national institution.

Dartmouth, though founded under the evangelical influence of Eleazar Wheelock, who used it as a base of operations for reaching the Indians with the gospel, did not have in its charter any official church connection. King's

College, later Columbia University, originated under Episcopalian control but in its charter chose not to go beyond "the great Principles of Christianity and Morality in which true Christians of each Denomination are generally agreed." Neither school had a strong enough "statement of faith" to protect it against the onslaughts to come.

Princeton's charter, on the other hand, insisted that its faculty be those who, among other things, were "convinced of the necessity of religious experience for salvation." It did not, however, require this of its students, though it seems most of the early students were born-again Christians, especially since at that time many of them were training for the ministry.

Again, the founders did not foresee the pressures to come. Yet it stood remarkably strong and for decades Christians looked to Princeton, long after, according to one observer, "Harvard and Yale had gone over to the enemy."

Yale President—Timothy Dwight meeting the students on their own ground.

But eventually Princeton too yielded to an ever-growing secular society.

Just how did this happen? Did the Princeton presidents capitulate? No. Though it may come as a surprise to many, every president from the school's founding in 1746 to the turn of the Twentieth Century seems to have been an evangelical Christian!

Did the trustees swing Princeton away from evangelical Christianity? No. Like the presidents, they held conservative until at least the turn of the Twentieth Century. They looked anxiously for any signs of unorthodox drift, especially in the teaching of science, where, for instance, the fad of Darwinian evolution might gain a toehold. Unfortunately, some administrators did finally begin to concede in this area.

But the real pressures ultimately came from the alumni.

Recall that Princeton's charter did not *require* that every student be a Christian. As Princeton grew into a large, full-fledged educational institution it turned out more and more non-Christian alumni, intent on a secular lifestyle. They could also give or withhold, donations. Eventually these

rose up and demanded a voice in the college's management and educational policies.

Only then was Princeton's high echelon forced to move from its evangelical thrust.

Though the Ivy League schools eventually turned secular, they fed into the mainstream of society in those early days a great army of graduates who could claim Jesus Christ as personal Savior and Lord, and who left a strong impact on our nation. Their presidents and their faculties helped to set a high spiritual tone, and at times their campuses in turn felt the impact of revival.

In fact, a remarkable movement of God commonly called "The First Great Awakening" took root under the preaching of a former Yale graduate and later Princeton president by the name of Jonathan Edwards.

Most historians agree that Jonathan Edwards stands with Benjamin Franklin as "one of the two outstanding minds in the America of the eighteenth century." Writes biographer Courtney Anderson, "Many believe that in another environment he could have become a scientist greater than Franklin. Certainly as a philosopher and theologian he had no peer in his own time."

The First Baptist church in America, Providence, Rhode Island.

Edwards entered Yale at thirteen and graduated valedictorian at seventeen. As he grew in his Christian faith at Yale he became somewhat of a "mystic," in the better sense, in his quest to know more of God. For example, he cites how, on one occasion, he was overwhelmed by reading the words of 1 Timothy 1:17: "Now unto the King eternal, immortal, invisible, the only wise God, be honor and glory for ever and ever, Amen."

"As I read the words, there came into my soul, and was as it were diffused through it, a sense of the glory of the Divine Being; a new sense, quite different from anything I ever experienced before ... I thought with myself, how excellent a Being that was, and how happy I should be, if I might enjoy that God ... and be as it were swallowed up in him for ever!

"From about that time, I began to have a new kind of apprehensions and ideas of Christ, and the work of redemption, and the glorious way of salvation by him ... God's excellency, his wisdom, his purity and love, seemed to appear in every thing; in the sun, moon, and stars; in the clouds, and blue sky; in

## Edwards left the pulpit, worked among the Indians, then eventually became president of Princeton.

the grass, flowers, trees; in the water, and all nature; which used greatly to fix my mind."

Edwards fell in love with a prominent young Christian lady, Sarah Pierrepont, who was noted for her charm, her flashing wit and a joyous repartee. She proved the ideal pastor's wife for Edwards, who took over his father-in-law's prestigious pulpit in Northhampton, Massachusetts, two years after their marriage.

The Edwardses eventually raised a remarkably fine family of eleven children. One writer describes the hospitality of the Edwards as "amazing to us with our more isolated family life. There might be a dozen to eighteen at dinner after a meeting. Guests sometimes stayed for weeks. If they fell ill, they had to be cared for until they were well. They came on horseback, and the horses had to be stabled and cared for. When a guest left, Jonathan usually rode a few miles with him to see him well on his way."

Edwards came to Northhampton at a time when spirituality was at a low ebb. The conditions he describes among the young people might sound much like conditions of today:

"Licentiousness for some years greatly prevailed among the youth of the town; there were many of them very much addicted to night walking and frequenting the tavern, and lewd practices wherein some by their example exceedingly corrupted others. It was their manner to get together in assemblies of both sexes, for mirth and jollity, which they called frolics; and they would often spend the greater part of the night in them, without regard to order in the families they belong to; indeed family government did too much fail in the town."

Then revival began—in 1734, while Jonathan Edwards was preaching a series of sermons on justification by faith alone. Conversions began, first the young, then their elders. A notorious young woman was saved. It was like a "flash of lightening" to the young people.

There were those who agonized, and those who rejoiced. Wrote Edwards: "... in the spring and summer following, anno 1735, the town seemed to be full of the presence of God; it never was so full of love, nor of joy, and yet so full of distress, as it was then."

By 1736 Edward's church had three hundred new converts, and news of the revival had spread throughout New England.

It took a new surge when George Whitefield arrived from England in 1740 for two years of evangelism in America. Whitefield had already risen to prominence as a key figure in the Wesleyan revivals underway in England—a great movement of God there

**Jonathan Edwards stands with Benjamin Franklin as one of the two outstanding minds in the America of the eighteenth century.**

triggered by a group of Christian students at Oxford University.

In those days evangelists did not enjoy the advantage of microphones, but Whitefield didn't need one. At Bristol, England, he had preached to 20,000 at one gathering and all could hear. In America he preached to five thousand on Boston Common and eight thousand at once in the fields.

In New England the revival reached its peak in 1741, and it was in July at Enfield, Massachusetts, that Edwards preached his most famous sermon, "Sinners in the Hands of an Angry God." Literally millions, myself included, first read this classic in a high school or college literature text. It might come as a surprise to many that he did not deliver this sermon in what some would describe as loud "hellfire and damnation" style. Edwards did not raise his voice nor even move his arms, though his typically good diction and enunciation made every word ring clear. As he hammered home the judgment of God, point upon point, each listener felt the impact of his own guilt.

Was this really the same Jonathan Edwards who spoke so frequently on the love, and grace, and beauty and majesty of God?

Yes, because Edwards became convinced that one could not really understand the great love of God until he also understood the awfulness of sin.

There was such conviction of sin that Edwards had to wait some time until the congregation quieted down. He finally prayed, descended from the pulpit and discoursed with the people. They closed with a hymn and dismissed.

During little more than two years, from 1740 to 1742, some 25,000 to 50,000 people were added to the New England churches, out of a total population of only 300,000! The movement changed the entire moral tone of New England for the better and justly earned the name of a "Great Awakening."

AS GOD CHOSE JONATHAN EDwards to launch the awakening throughout New England, he put his hand on Gilbert Tennant as his chief instrument to spread the revival through New Jersey, Pennsylvania and the middle colonies.

Who was Gilbert Tennant?

The oldest son of a Presbyterian minister in remote Neshaminy, Bucks County, Pennsylvania. His father, William Tennant, singlehandedly schooled Gilbert in his own home to be a minister. But the younger sons also needed an education, so he built a log cabin in his yard to use as a school. Here he taught his sons—and fifteen others— the languages, logic, theology, and also imparted to them an evangelical passion which sent them out flaming evan-

George Whitefield

gelists.

Gilbert Tennant, his brothers and their handful of dedicated young associates saw conversions wherever they preached, and revival began to spread throughout the middle colonies. But it also triggered conflict. Presbyterian ministers up and down the land were divided, some for the revival (the "New Lights"), some against it (the "Old Lights"). The latter looked down their noses at William Tennant's "Log College" and branded his graduates "half-educated enthusiasts" (though two of them eventually became presidents of Princeton!).

Strong dissent threatened to abort genuine revival, but enter once again George Whitefield. The spontaneous movement in the middle colonies had erupted independently of the one triggered in New England by Jonathan Edwards, but Whitefield helped bring the two together. He could back anyone who preached conversion, regardless of party label.

On one occasion, preaching from the balcony of the courthouse in Philadelphia, Whitefield cried out: "Father Abraham, whom have you in Heaven? Any Episcopalians? *'No.'* Any Presbyterians? *'No.'* Have you any Independents or Seceders? *'No.'* Have you any Methodists? *'No, no, no!!'* Whom have you there? *'We don't know those names here. All who are here are Christians-believers in Christ-men who have overcome by the blood of the Lamb and the word of his testimony.'* Oh, is this the case? Then God help us, God help us all, to forget party names, and to become Christians in deed and in truth."

In time the revival-minded churches triumphed. They grew and multiplied. Young people crowded their pews. The other churches dwindled, lost ground and drew mostly the elderly.

Meanwhile, the revival spread into Virginia and the southern colonies—in three stages.

Samuel Davies, one of the "Log College" graduates who eventually became

Baptists and Methodists followed the frontier.

president of the College of New Jersey (later Princeton), planted the first phase.

But then two Baptists, Shubal Stearns and his brother-in-law, Daniel Marshall, emerged—both products of the New England awakening. Under their grassroots preaching, revival seemed to explode through Virginia and into North Carolina—especially around the Sandy Creek region in Guilford County. The Baptists faced much persecution, but the more they patiently withstood it, the more they grew.

Also, many came to see that Baptist notions of separation and independence were in harmony with the political philosophy of the American Revolutionary leaders. For paying taxes to the Established Church appeared much

like taxation without representation. The ten-year growth of the Separate Baptists, from 1765 to 1775, is almost unparalleled in Baptist history.

Devereux Jarratt, an evangelical Anglican turned Methodist in spirit, fanned the revival's third phase in the southern colonies. Suddenly Methodists, like the Baptists, sprang up everywhere. Circuit riders spread the Good News, and Virginia-North Carolina became the cradle of Methodism.

Such movements of God were not to be the last in the history of early America. But that is another story.

THE IVY LEAGUE COLLEGES OF an earlier era, though small by today's standards, turned out a long parade of graduates who rose to promi-

Noah Webster at work on his dictionary.

nence in law, politics, education, and other fields. To no small extent they shaped the heart and mind of America during its formative years.

One of the names most remembered today is Noah Webster—simply because his name has endured along with his dictionary still used (updated many times, of course) by millions.

A graduate of Yale, Webster achieved distinction in many arenas. He practiced law in Hartford, launched a daily newspaper in New York, helped establish Amherst College and routinely rubbed shoulders with men like George Washington, Alexander Hamilton and John Jay.

But the biggest segment of his life—thirty six years of it, in fact—he dedicated to the Herculean task of producing his *American Dictionary.*

Like a human computer, Webster systematized in his mind, and in his huge files of clippings, almost every piece of knowledge he acquired. He meticulously researched everything from the cause of Asiatic cholera to the reasons for a seeming change in the American climate. But he specialized in pursuing the etymology of words.

No less a person could have ever completed the mammoth task he had undertaken—and done it right. Even then English speech was changing rapidly from year to year, with new discoveries in science, new political terms

An early American schoolhouse.

and a myriad of other forces upon the language.

At one point in the project, Webster suspended his labors on defining words and devoted a number of years on a related pursuit—tracing the origin of the English language and its connection with those of other countries. He researched the vocabularies of twenty of the principal languages of the world, and made a synopisis of the most important words in each.

Webster, after his extensive research on the origin of language, sharply opposed the evolutionary concept that language *evolved* along with the progressive development of animal life—from grunts to groans.

He wrote, in his *Introduction to an American Dictionary of the English Language, 1856:* "... We read, that God brought to Adam the fowls and beasts he had made, and that Adam gave them names; and that when his female companion was made, he gave her a name. After the eating of the forbidden fruit, it is stated that God addressed Adam and Eve, reproving them for their disobedience, and pronouncing the penalties which they had incurred. In the account of these transactions, it is further related that Adam and Eve both replied to their Maker, and excused their disobedience.

"If we admit, what is the literal and obvious interpretation of this narrative, that vocal sounds or words were used in these communications between God and the progenitors of the human race, it results that Adam was not only endowed with intellect for understanding his Maker, or the signification of words, but was furnished both with the faculty of speech and with speech itself, or the knowledge and use of words as signs of ideas, and this before the formation of the woman. Hence we may infer that language was bestowed on Adam, in the same manner as all his other faculties and knowledge, by supernatural power; or, in other words, was of divine origin. It is, therefore, probably, that language, as well as the faculty of speech, was the immediate Gift of God."

Here Webster obviously applied a Christian perspective to his study of languages. From his youth he respected religion, took a high view on the inspiration of the Scriptures and set out from Yale to pursue a course of virtue through life—to perform every moral social duty with scrupulous exactness.

But at age forty he began to confide that perhaps he was resting his beliefs more on his accomplishments than on the simple grace of God. He had been earnest in his endeavors and active for social good. But was this enough?

At this point he took up an earnest study of the Bible, with the same meticulous care and complete honesty that characterized the man himself. And as he advanced, his objections to the gospel fell one by one, and one evening he cast himself down before God, confessed his sins and implored pardon through the merits of the Redeemer alone.

The next morning he called his family together and, with deep emotion, told them that for years he had neglected one of his most important duties as their parent and head—family prayer. After reading the Scriptures he led his family to the throne of grace—a habit he continued until his death years later. He made a public profession in April, 1808, and three daughters soon followed with decisions of their own.

Webster continued in his study of the Scriptures over the years, despite the demands on his time in completing the *American Dictionary,* and certain definitions in those earlier editions reflect his Christian stance.

The tall, slender Noah Webster walked with a light and elastic step until the time of his death at 85. As he faced the close of life on earth, Webster quoted to a friend the words of the apostle Paul: "I know whom I have believed, and am persuaded that He is able to keep that which I have committed unto him against that day."

## CHAPTER SIX

# WESTWARD INTO THE WILDERNESS

AT THE CLOSE OF THE Revolutionary War the United States boundary was extended westward to the Mississippi River. But except along the eastern seaboard, the nation was one vast wilderness. Even along the Atlantic, great stretches of remote countryside separated the narrow line of settlements. Just four million people showed up on the first general census in 1790.

Then the westward migration began.

One stream—made up mostly of New Englanders—pushed out along the valley of the Mohawk. A second one moved through southern Pennsylvania, Maryland and the Cumberland Gap. A third stream drifted through the Valley of Virginia and over the passes of the Blue Ridge Mountains into Kentucky and Tennessee.

Then southern Ohio opened, especially after General Wayne defeated the Miami Confederacy at the Battle of Fallen Timbers. Soon the Ohio River itself became the great highway to the West. The migration accelerated following passage of the embargo of 1808. Roads swarmed with wagons, cattle, sheep, horses. One European observed in 1817, "All America seems to be breaking up and moving westward."

As many pulled up roots and moved out onto the frontier, they left behind their churches—if they had any. The wilderness demanded everything of them—just to survive. They had to clear land, build cabins, struggle with crops. The frontier brought out the best in some, but the worst in others, especially those who had neglected religion.

In all of this, what happened to the churches—and the major denominations entrenched on the Eastern seaboard? Some woke up a few decades later to realize they had been left in the dust of the Westward getaway. Other

Francis Asbury and wagon party at Cumberland Gap.

movements, though, flourished—far beyond expectations. Who prospered, and who did not? What made the difference? The story of what happened as our nation pushed open the frontier carries many lessons even for today.

Church figures in a current U.S. Almanac show that Baptists today (all groups) far outnumber any other Protestant segment (nearly 27 million) and Methodists rank second (12.7 million).

The Anglicans (later Episcopalians) and Congregationalists started out on the American scene in favored position. Both enjoyed numerical superiority and the status of being the established church in several of the colonies. They had the inside track. In 1700, for instance, the Anglican and Congregational churches outnumbered Baptist and Presbyterian churches 4-1, and at that time the Methodist church did not even exist!

What factors contributed specifically to the Baptist success story? For one thing, their independent form of gov-

ernment harmonized completely with the new and thriving American democracy. Indeed, Baptist input, in various ways, had helped to create that democracy. In contrast, Anglicans lived under the cloud of the Revolution. Much of the Anglican clergy fled to England when the Revolutionary War broke out, and it took decades for the church to recover. When the Anglican Church finally reorganized as the Episcopal Church, much of the impetus came from those states where it had not been "the established church."

But there is much more to the Baptist story. Unlike the entrenched churches of New England, when the frontier opened, Baptists moved with the people. Recall that the revival fires of the First Great Awakening had already multiplied Baptist numbers, especially in Virginia and North Carolina. And these states in particular poured streams of settlers over the mountains into the frontier during the closing decades of the eighteenth cen-

tury.

Often whole congregations moved westward. One example was the Gilbert's Creek Church in Kentucky, which trekked west in one body with its pastor, Lewis Craig. The congregation moved together over the mountains, the pastor continued services as they camped along the way, and baptized new believers in the clear mountain streams. American church historian William Warren Sweet describes the scene:

"On their march westward they heard the news of the surrender of Cornwallis at Yorktown and made the hills ring with the firing of their rifles in their glad rejoicings. Finally reaching the place of their new settlement in December, 1781, they gathered for worship 'around the same old Bible they had used back in Spottsylvanie,' in Virginia."

The "farmer-preacher" played a big role in the rapid Baptist growth on the frontier. Writes Howard Whaley in "The Church in America" series in *Moody Monthly:*

"The Baptist 'farmer-preacher,' ordained or licensed to preach, took up farming right along with the other frontiersmen. He cleared and worked his land like the rest of his neighbors, became the shepherd of the little Baptist flock and conducted the 'religious meetin's' on Sundays or as the need arose.

"Many of these farmer-preachers, although lacking formal education and salaried positions, were greatly used of God as they 'exercised their gifts' in the ministry. Typical was Joab Powell (1799-1873), a Tennessean who preached for twenty years in Missouri as a farmer-preacher and then moved on to Oregon.

"Such men as Powell, Lewis Craig, William Marshall and John Taylor saw to it that the settler heard the gospel and that churches were formed all along the frontier. Through the effective use of laymen, the farmer-preacher, circuit riders, revivalism and a direct appeal of men with a simple Bible-centered message, the Baptists by 1850 had grown to be second only to the Methodists, with some 9,375 churches established."

Almost all the early frontier Baptist churches took their names from creeks, valleys, rivers or some other nearby geographical feature. It might be Clear Creek, or Big Crossing, or Limestone. Many churches started with no more than six to ten members, with the average about twenty. The first meeting-house might be constructed of round logs. A decade or two later, if the church prospered, the congregation would undertake a new "building program"—this time with hewn logs, a fireplace and brick chimney. Abraham Lincoln's father, Thomas Lincoln, helped to build a Baptist church like this in Pigeon Creek, Indiana, in 1819.

Though Baptists would eventually overtake them, the early Methodists established themselves as front-runners in bringing the gospel to the frontier. Whaley nicely capsules what happened:

"The Methodists," he says, "laid the foundation for success when they adapted to the social structure of the frontier, trained Christian laymen and adopted the circuit system from Wesley in England.

"Moreover, they moved with the frontier and zealously preached a simple gospel of free grace which found ready acceptance among the hardened frontiersmen. Through effective preachers like Francis Asbury, Thomas Coke, William McKendree, Jesse Lee and others, the Methodists were soon winning thousands of converts and spreading revival. By 1830 they numbered over half a million and by the mid-nineteenth century they had grown to be the leading denomination in most of the states.

"Beginning with a toehold and ending with a meeting house sums up their success. But success was the result of great leadership, dogged pursuit of the 'sinner' and faithful dedication. 'Nobody was out but cows and the Methodist preachers,' went a frontier saying to describe bad weather. Such was their reputation for devotion to duty and exposure to personal hardships and dangers. And for the most part they were thorough, as the following testimony of a Presbyterian missionary in Kentucky attests:

" 'I at length became ambitious to find a family whose cabin had not been entered by a Methodist preacher. In several days I travelled from settlement to settlement but into every hovel I entered I learned that the Methodist missionary had been there before me.' "

Nor were the Methodist frontier preachers content simply to follow up their own people. Their philosophy was, "We don't *find* Methodists on the

frontier, we *make* them."

N O PIONEER PREACHER, if indeed any American frontiersman, traveled so many miles through the wilderness in one lifetime, nor endured such hardships, as did the incredible Methodist circuit rider, Francis Asbury. An Englishman by birth who worked as a blacksmith, Asbury became a Christian at 16. When John Wesley called for volunteer evangelists, Asbury set sail for the American colonies in 1771, just five years before the birth of the American nation.

When the Revolutionary war broke out, Wesley and his missionaries promptly retreated to their native England. All, that is, except Francis Asbury. He saw a job to do, and at heart he was already too much a part of the American scene to abandon its land and its people. He developed a strong love and patriotism for the new nation. His high regard for George Washington, whom he knew personally, was exceeded perhaps only by his admiration of John Wesley. When the war ceased, he intensified his consuming passion to evangelize the American wilderness—a task that would stretch over forty-four years and an astounding number of miles.

Though a robust man on the one hand, Asbury suffered from one chronic ailment after another—so much

Emigration—Encampment at night

so that one biographer calls him a "Job of old on horseback." Migraine headaches plagued him throughout his life, and chronic throat infections would become so severe that doctors feared he would strangle. He wrestled with malaria, asthma, pneumonia, rheumatism, high fevers and other diseases, and in his mid-forties he plunged onward convinced he could not live another year. But he died at 71.

*The Journal and Letters of Francis Asbury,* a terse daily diary which Asbury kept as he traveled his circuit of some nineteen states, gives us some feel of the life that became almost routine. On his long circuit out of West Virginia into Maryland and Pennsylvania in June, 1784, Asbury wrote:

"Although my body is weak, my soul is filled with love to God ... We began to ascend the Alleghany ... keeping the route of Braddock's road for about twenty-two miles, along a rough pathway: arriving at a small house and halting for the night, we had, literally to lie as thick as three in a bed."

And in April of 1790, from Kentucky, where he saw the graves of twenty-four men and women who had been slain by Indians:

"We are now in a house in which a man was killed by savages; ... I consider myself in danger; but my God will keep me whilst thousands pray for me." Often he found himself "strangely outdone for want of sleep, having been greatly deprived of it in my journey through the wilderness; which is like being at sea, in some respects, and in others worse. Our way is over mountains, steep hills, deep rivers, and muddy creeks; a thick growth of reeds for miles together; and no inhabitants but wild beasts and savage men ... we ate no regular meal; our bread grew short, and I was much spent."

With his incredible travels which spanned more than four decades, Asbury, perhaps more than any other man, saw firsthand the early nation unfold. He saw the untouched regions beyond the Appalachians (which he called "the American Alps") as lands of future progress and exclaimed in 1803 as he looked over Ohio, "What will not

## The incredible Francis Asbury
## rode a quarter million miles on horseback
## and preached some 25,000 sermons!

a little enterprise do for a man in this highly favored country!" The next year in Tennessee he saw the crowds of people moving toward the fertile West and predicted that despite sufferings and hardship, "In ten years, I think, the new State will be one of the most flourishing in the Union."

His journal records the natural wonders of the new nation. In West Virginia Asbury visited a cave where he saw "some of the greatest natural curiosities my eyes ever beheld ..." and in one lofty underground chamber he sang *Still Out of the Deepest Abyss* and described the sound as "wonderful."

He prayed and sang in the caves, in the valleys, and on the mountaintops. He preached, prayed, and sang in homes, courthouses, barns and churches. He was a Johnny Appleseed of the gospel, planting here and there, returning year after year to an abundant harvest. He travelled perhaps more than 250,000 miles, preached some 25,000 sermons, and may have written around 50,000 letters!

Perhaps because so many knew him and were praying for him, Asbury always seemed to remain unscathed. At the outset of his career he survived a violent sickness on the seas enroute from England. During the Revolutionary War he remained free from arrest, seemingly an Englishman accepted by the "enemy," and, in the words of one observer, "a lone rider molested on a thousand wilderness trails by neither Indians or bandits."

Asbury set an unbelievable pace for himself, and over his more than forty years of itinerate evangelism he averaged two sermons a day! An excellent administrator, though sometimes dictatorial, he was continually exhorting his force of circuit riders, breaking ground for new churches, scurrying from one important meeting to another. He studied the Bible fervently, but also read other books. He arose early and accomplished so much that, were he on earth today, he might well be sought after to conduct seminars on management and use of time. When Asbury arrived in America in 1771, the Methodists numbered no more than a thousand. When he died in 1816, there were 214,000. Little wonder that he became the first Methodist Bishop in America, a title, incidentally, that John Wesley deplored.

Journalist Herman B. Teeter aptly summed up Asbury's contribution to America:

"The names of Daniel Boone, Davy Crockett, Kit Carson, and Jim Bowie are well known in history and legend. Not so that of Francis Asbury. Yet the ex-blacksmith from England outlasted and outdistanced them all. He knew more hardship and physical suffering, but sought no personal fortune, no

(pgs. 104 & 105) A circuit rider calls on a family in the wilderness.

acclaim, no territory. Year after year he gathered behind him a growing army of hard-riding, hard-preaching men who, like himself, would never know comfort or riches.

"He must have faced more inclement weather in one year than most men brave in a lifetime ... His horses fell beneath him, or ran away with him. But people were his main concern. To him they were souls to be saved ... Asbury did the job he set out to do, and in his old age his passing to and fro across the land found thousands gathering for a glimpse of him. 'People call me by name as they pass me on the road, and I hand them a religious tract in German or English; or I call at a door for a glass of water, and leave a little pamphlet.'

"He never had a home of his own. He had no address other than 'America,' but sooner or later a letter so addressed would reach him.

"Today highways and railways crisscross the large slice of the United States that was Asbury country. Fly over it in a jet plane and look down on this vast area, once uncivilized and virtually uncharted. Even from 30,000 feet it stretches out of sight beyond every horizon. Try driving though Asbury country for 5,000 miles—a typical annual circuit for the pioneer bishop—and consider what it would be like to make the same trip by horseback, sulky, chaise, and afoot!"

Asbury lamented the tendency of the early Methodist preachers to stay "shut up" in cities along the Eastern seaboard. He vowed at the outset to train up a whole new generation of men—both preachers and laymen—who would follow the new westward population trends and who would move among those people where the spiritual vacuum seemed greatest.

The man, his method and his mission set forth an example that Twentieth Century Christians might well follow today.

THE PRESBYTERIANS also made their impact on the frontier, though their numerical growth proved not as spectacular. They established an early foothold, for instance, in southwestern Pennsylvania near Pittsburgh, and also near Lexington, Tennessee. They also profited from a "Plan of Union" proposed by the son of Jonathan Edwards and adopted in 1801. It provided that Congregational and Presbyterian settlers in a new community could form one congregation and

call a minister of either denomination. But because few Congregational ministers showed up on the frontier scene, in almost every case it worked to the advantage of the Presbyterians. Many churches which began as Congregational soon became Presbyterian.

Why did they not grow, though, like the Baptists and Methodists?

For one thing, they more or less settled for reaching people of their own Presbyterian background (though with notable exceptions).

Presbyterians had a rather slow process of establishing congregations and calling ministers. Methodist circuit riders proved "Johnny-on-the-spot," ready to start a Bible class or a church almost as soon as they arrived. And Baptists often beat even the Methodists, for their farmer-preachers came with the people!

Too, Presbyterian preaching tended to be more theological. Frontier settlers looked for practical preaching, and usually also for more emotion.

Many Presbyterian ministers became schoolteachers, which siphoned off the clergy. On the other hand, it put Presbyterians into the forefront of frontier education—including higher education—and thereby gave them an influence far beyond their numbers.

So went the churches who were in on the ground floor of our nation's religious heritage. But from whence came all the other denominations?

Many were basically ethnic in origin. Significant numbers of the Dutch Reformed had settled in upper New York state. Moravians, Quakers and Mennonites clustered in Pennsylvania and New Jersey. As immigrants poured in from Europe, other groups came into prominence—the Lutherans from Germany and Scandinavia, the various Swedish groups, and large numbers of Roman Catholics.

Also, the general freedom and independence of the frontier allowed thousands to free themselves of church hierachy and to handle things—even Christian affairs—in a way the common people best saw fit. Inevitably, this also led to schisms, new denominations, even cults.

Some churches split for good reasons, some not so good. In some

cases strong-minded individuals wandered off on some biblically-false tangent and went out, with their followers, to propagate it. In other cases, particularly as older-line churches strayed from the gospel, concerned Christians separated themselves on grounds of apostasy.

Despite the cults the frontier might have helped produce, its freedom of spirit and its independent climate helped establish a precedence for the "grassroots" Christianity which is thriving within evangelicalism today. These churches do not rely simply on the clergy to do the job, but permit, indeed encourage, everyone to get involved and to reach out to others in their own culture. Our nation today would be much the poorer had not at least some of the common people in those days learned how to personally take up the faith and "pass it on."

WHEN THOUSANDS of colonial Americans began to pull up roots and head West, conditions did not exactly produce a nation of churchgoers. Even before the Revolution, an agnosticism imported in part from Europe had taken its toll. Many had succumbed to the writings of men like Voltaire and Thomas Paine, however full of flaws was their logic. By the turn of the 18th Century Unitarianism had all but swept New England and the Atlantic seaboard—especially eastern Massachusetts—from which it has

A camp meeting on the frontier.

never yet fully recovered.

The religion of many who headed West left something to be desired, and even good church members, once out into the frontier, forsook their churches. Life became tough and rough; morals declined. One writer describes the scene aptly: "Corn liquor flowed freely; marriages were celebrated long after children had arrived; gun and rope settled far too many legal disputes. The West was crowded with Sabbath-breakers and profane swearers, thieves, murderers and blasphemers, with neither courts of law nor public opinion to raise a rebuke."

Colonial Christians who cared about the souls of men and the future of the country saw the peril clearly. If such a spiritual drift continued among the thousands of settlers already in the Alleghanies and beyond, it could bring down the judgment of God upon the entire nation. Yet only a thin system of trails and waterways connected the colonies with that vast wilderness beyond the mountains. Humanly speaking, it seemed an impossible task for godly men to change the course of events.

But God intervened in a mighty event now known as the Second Great Awakening, which helped reverse the spiritual skid and surely saved America from calamity.

Where did it start?

Some point to James McGready, an

Today's mass evangelism has its
roots in the frontier camp meeting.

angular, black-eyed Scotch-Irishman
born on the Pennsylvania frontier, and
a graduate of one of the "log cabin colleges" like the one which produced the
men who sparked the First Great
Awakening.

McGready, a Presbyterian, first set
out to evangelize in North Carolina.
He pulled no punches, preaching
against deadness in the churches and
calling on frontiersmen to give up
strong drink. But many rough-and-
tough settlers wanted their drink and
did not want lectures from men of the
cloth (in actuality ministers wore
buckskin, says one authority, and "took
their turn with the next man at hoeing
corn or splitting kindling.")

McGready finally decided to move
on to Kentucky where he pastored
three small congregations in Logan
County. This was no pushover territory

either. Most knew the region as a
notorious hangout for all kinds of law-
breakers and unsavory characters. But
under McGready's zealous, forthright
preaching, God began to work.

Before long several other Presbyterian and Methodist preachers joined
McGready to spread what seemed at
least to be a small revival in the making.
It picked up momentum and emotion.
During a service at Gasper River in
1799 as McGready preached the
realities of Heaven and Hell, many fell
to the ground and lay "powerless,
groaning, praying and crying for
mercy." Women screamed and tough
men sobbed like children. Later during
a meeting at Red River as Methodist
preacher John McGee "shouted and
exhorted with all possible energy,"
numbers professed conversion. It was
here that the great western revival be-

## The Second Great Awakening reversed a spiritual skid that surely saved America from calamity.

gan, which came to be known as the Logan County, or Cumberland, revival.

As word spread, Kentuckians from as far as one hundred miles threaded their way to the meetings in Logan County. The crowds grew, and soon visitors had to camp out for one, two or three nights. The historical "camp meeting" suddenly emerged. Men chopped down more trees to accommodate the crowds, and arranged split-log benches into a veritable "church-in-the-wilderness."

The high emotional pitch of the meetings, in part peculiar to the frontier culture, eventually triggered no small controversy—especially among the more staid clergy of the East. But the movement grew.

Barton W. Stone, a Presbyterian minister from nearby Bourbon County, showed up to view the meetings and make his own judgment. He returned convinced it was a genuine work of God and soon touched off in Bourbon County the most famous gathering of the Second Great Awakening—the Cane Ridge meeting. It extended over several days of August, 1801, and drew crowds estimated as high as 25,000.

One eyewitness describes the scene:

"I attended with eighteen Presbyterian ministers; and Baptist and Methodist preachers, I do not know how many; all being either preaching or exhorting the distressed with more harmony than could be expected. The governor of our State was with us and encouraging the work... They are commonly collected in small circles of ten or twelve, closely adjoining another circle and all engaged in singing Watt's and Hart's hymns; and then a minister steps upon a stump or log, and begins an exhortation or sermon, when as many as can hear collect around him."

Another description of the impressive scene at night:

"The glare of the blazing camp-fires falling on a dense assemblage ... and reflected back from long ranges of tents upon every side; hundreds of candles and lamps suspended among the trees, together with numerous torches flashing to and fro, throwing an uncertain light upon the tremulous foliage, and giving an appearance of dim and indefinite extent to the depth of the forest; the solemn chanting of hymns swelling and falling on the night wind; the impassioned exhortations; the earnest prayers; the sobs, shrieks, or shouts, bursting from persons under intense agitation of mind, the sudden spasms which seize upon scores, and unexpectedly dashed them to the ground; all conspired to invest the scene with terrific interest ..."

Despite emotional excesses, many not described here, the revival movement spread and had a profound effect in transforming the lives and morals of western society. Thousands were swept into churches. Between 1800 and 1803 more than 10,000 were added to the Baptist churches in Kentucky alone.

Wrote one observer: "Upon the whole, I think the revival in Kentucky the most extraordinary that has ever visited the church of Christ; and all things considered, it was peculiarly adapted to the circumstances of the country into which it came."

The revival and its effects eventually spread beyond the Kentucky borders. Moreover, it established the camp meeting as a legitimate Protestant innovation that helped bring the gospel to the masses. The Methodists in particular adopted it and staged more than one thousand camp meetings throughout the frontier. But they were not replicas of Cane Ridge. Bernard A. Weisberger, associate professor of history at Wayne State University, observes:

"They were combed, washed, and made respectable. Permanent sites were picked, regular dates chosen, and preachers and flocks given ample time to prepare. When meeting time came, the arriving worshippers in their wagons were efficiently taken in charge, told where to park their vehicles and pasture their teams, and given a spot for their tents ...

"Tight scheduling kept the worship moving according to plan—dawn prayers, eight o'clock sermons, eleven o'clock sermons, dinner breaks, afternoon prayers and sermons, meals, again, and candlelight services. Years of experience tightened the schedules, and camp meeting manuals embodied the fruits of practice. Regular hymns replaced the discordant bawling of the primitive era. Things took on a generally homelike look.

"There were ladies who did not hesitate to bring their best feather beds to spread in the tents, and meals tended to be planned and ample affairs. Hams, turkeys, gravies, biscuits, preserves, and melons produced contented worshippers and happy memories. There were new rules to cope with disorderliness as well. Candles, lamps and torches fixed to trees kept the area well lit ..."

Not that there was a total lack of enthusiasm. Hymns were still yelled and stamped as much as sung. Nor was it out of bounds for the audience to pepper the sermons with shouts of "Amen!" and "Glory!"

In later years such gatherings took on other forms. The camp meeting, in fact, laid the foundations of mass evangelism—and the campaigns later assembled by such men as Dwight L. Moody, Charles Finney, Billy Sunday and Billy Graham. The camp meeting of those times helped to reverse America's destiny and eventually channelled thousands into the churches.

Its offsprings are still at work today.

CHAPTER SEVEN

# ABRAHAM LINCOLN: "IF THE ALMIGHTY RULER OF NATIONS ..."

THE YEAR, 1863. The United States of America, still less than one hundred years old, faced its greatest crisis. A great civil war threatened to destroy the Union as armies of the North and South clashed across the Potomac from Washington D. C. and also to the southwest near Chatanooga, Tennessee.

The Senate called upon President Lincoln to set aside a national day of "fasting, humiliation and prayer." The President concurred and designated April 30. He urged both personal and national repentance.

"It is the duty of nations as well as of men," he said, "to own their dependence upon the overruling power of God, to confess their sins and transgressions, in humble sorrow, yet with assured hope that genuine repentance will lead to mercy and pardon; and to recognize the sublime truth, announced in the Holy Scriptures and proven by all history, that those nations only are blessed whose God is the Lord."

Lincoln's proclamation continued with an analysis of the country which rings strangely true of our nation today:

"We have been the recipients of the choicest bounties of Heaven. We have been preserved, these many years, in peace and prosperity. We have grown in numbers, wealth and power, as no other nation has ever grown. But we have forgotten God. We have forgotten the gracious hand which preserved us in peace, and multiplied and enriched and strengthened us; and we have vainly imagined, in the deceitfulness of our hearts, that all these blessings were produced by some superior wisdom and virtue of our own. Intoxicated with unbroken success, we have become too self-sufficient to feel the necessity of redeeming and preserving grace, too proud to pray to the God that made us!"

No other President so consistently demonstrated, and so deeply believed as did Abraham Lincoln that the Almighty God of the universe rules in the affairs of men. Lincoln once said to his register of the treasury, L. E. Chittenden:

"That the Almighty does make use of human agencies, and directly intervenes in human affairs, is one of the plainest statements of the Bible. I have had so many evidences of his direction, so many instances when I have been controlled by some other power than my own will, that I cannot doubt that this power comes from above."

The man who had just issued the Emancipation Proclamation concluded with the deep conviction, "I am confident that it is His design to restore the Union. He will do it in His own good time. We should obey and not oppose His will."

Even as a boy, Lincoln seemed to grasp the great truth that God directs history. But he did wrestle with certain other doctrines of the Christian faith, especially in the days when he served as a young lawyer in New Salem, Illinois. Was Abraham Lincoln an orthodox Christian? What did he really believe? Why did he never join a church? Did he fall short in his doctrine and believe in universal salvation—that ultimately Jesus Christ would save all men? And how did he regard the authority of the Bible?

Such questions about Abraham Lincoln have been researched, debated, explored, for years. Not everyone has come to the same conclusions. The fact that so many stories have been passed

on, not all of them well-founded, complicates the issue.

It is not my intent to try to settle the matter. But a brief overview of Lincoln's religious quest, together with a few excerpts from his days as President, at the very least overwhelms one with his obvious awareness of his need and dependence on One higher than himself.

From his boyhood log cabin days Lincoln learned to study and memorize the Scriptures, both from his mother and perhaps also from listening to sermons at the Pigeon Creek Baptist church. He once told a gathering of black people who had given him a costly Bible in Baltimore, "All the good Saviour gave to the world was communicated through this book. But for it we could not know right from wrong."

And on another occasion he told his treasurer Chittenden:

"The character of the Bible is easily established, at least to my satisfaction. We have to believe many things which we do not comprehend. The Bible is the only one that claims to be God's book—to comprise His law—His history. It contains an immense amount of evidence of its own authenticity ... I decided a long time ago that it was less difficult to believe that the Bible was what it claimed to be than to disbelieve it."

ABRAHAM LINCOLN knew his Bible well, and he could quote it with ease. The Scriptures permeate his speeches, not just as an adornment to impress others, but as an integral part of his logic. The biblical phrase, "a

**The Scriptures permeated Lincoln's speeches, not just as political adornment, but as an integral part of his logic.**

house divided against itself cannot stand," became his classic plea for preservation of the Union. His second inaugural address is filled with the flavor of King James rhetoric.

His acquaintance with Scripture came through even in humorous ways. Like the first day of the famous Lincoln-Douglas debates over the office of U.S. Senator from Illinois. Writes Clarence E. Macartney in *Lincoln and the Bible:*

"When Lincoln rose to take his turn and answer Douglas, the "Little Giant," whose first name was Stephen, he (Lincoln) took off his linen duster, which all travellers wore in that day, and, handing it to one of his backers on the platform, said in a voice which reached far out in the crowd about the stand: 'Hold my coat while I stone Stephen!'

"There were few in the thousands listening to Lincoln that day who did not recognize at once the allusion to the first martyr, Stephen, and how, when he was stoned, the witnesses laid down their clothes at a young man's feet, whose name was Saul."

But during his days in New Salem, Lincoln clearly struggled with his faith—or lack of it, and it seems evident that, at best, he held a view of universal salvation—from his misinterpretation of such verses as 1 Corinthians 15:22.

Because of this, perhaps, his political opponent for Congress at that time,

Methodist circuit rider Peter Cartwright, went so far as to label him an "infidel." The term was popular in those days, though often misused. Lincoln defended himself in a handbill to the editor of the *Illinois Gazette*. He denied he was an "open scoffer at Christianity" and, in fact, said he could not support a man for office whom he knew to be an open enemy of, and scoffer at, religion.

Biographer Carl Sandburg tells of another encounter, when Lincoln went to one of Cartwright's evangelistic meetings. At the invitation Cartwright asked those who wished to lead a new life and give their hearts to God to stand. A sprinkling of men, women and children stood.

"Then the preacher exhorted, 'All who do not wish to go to hell will stand.' All stood—except Lincoln.

"Then said Cartwright in his gravest voice, 'I observe that many responded to the first invitation to give their hearts to God and go to heaven. And I further observe that all of you save one indicated that you did not desire to go to

**Even as a boy Abraham Lincoln seemed to grasp the great truth that God directs history.**

hell. The sole exception is Mr. Lincoln, who did not respond to either invitation. May I inquire of you, Mr. Lincoln, where you are going?'

"And Lincoln slowly rose and slowly spoke, 'I came here as a respectful listener. I did not know that I was to be singled out by Brother Cartwright. I believe in treating religious matters with due solemnity. I admit that the questions propounded by Brother Cartwright are of great importance. I did not feel called upon to answer as the rest did. Brother Cartwright asks me directly where I am going. I desire to reply with equal directness: I am going to Congress.' The meeting broke up."

Throughout his life Abraham Lincoln did not join a church. Nor did he care for creeds. He preferred to draw his convictions directly from the Scriptures rather than from what he regarded as man-made abstracts.

Shortly after the Lincolns lost their son, Edward, in death, Mary Todd Lincoln joined the First Presbyterian Church in Springfield, Illinois, by profession of faith. The minister there at that time, a Dr. James Smith, gave Lincoln a book he had written called *The Christian's Defense*—on the evidence of Christianity and the arguments for the authority of the Scriptures. As a lawyer Lincoln examined the evidence for several weeks and reported back that he found it convincing. Smith asserts Lin-

coln was genuinely converted at that point, but later evidence does not confirm this.

IT IS UNMISTAKABLE, however, that Abraham Lincoln's spiritual convictions deepened as he assumed the awesome role of President and faced the agonizing dilemmas of the slavery issue and a civil war.

The slavery question troubled Lincoln immensely. He firmly saw it as a moral evil, an injustice that would surely bring the wrath of God upon the nation. Common sense, coupled with the Bible he so frequently read, drove

New Salem

him to these conclusions. Yet there were those who, from the same Scriptures, insisted that the Bible did not specifically condemn slavery. They pointed to its existence both in the Old and New Testament ... that slaves were enjoined to be obedient to their masters, and that Paul himself sent the fugitive slave Onesimus back to his master Philemon at Colosse.

But Lincoln observed that the kind of slavery that existed in the culture of those times involved no racial overtones. It was the slavery of white men. Would not the advocates of slavery in America maintain that the slavery of a black man was right, but the slavery of a white man wrong? And he wondered how a society could do to a whole race of men as they would have no man do unto themselves.

Yet Lincoln acknowledged that many Southerners themselves wanted earnestly to resolve the problem in due time. They also sincerely wanted to guard states' rights, as did Lincoln, and he said that if it had been the problem of people in the North, they would probably have responded no differently than had the South.

Who, then, was right? Lincoln's first inaugural address, March 4, 1861, expressed a deep conviction that the God of history would overrule impending events to bring about His will.

"If the Almighty Ruler of Nations," he said, "with His eternal truth and justice, be on your side of the North, or on yours of the South, that truth and that justice will surely prevail by the judgment of this great tribunal of the American people.

"Intelligence, patriotism, Christianity, and a firm reliance on Him who has never yet forsaken this favored land, are still competent to adjust in the best way, all our present difficulty."

Four years later, with the outcome of the Civil War tilting in favor of the Union, he once more hammered home, in his second inaugural address, the truth that "The Almighty has His own purposes."

In office Lincoln seemed to turn ever more to the Bible and to prayer. And with Lincoln it came from the depths of his soul. Any attempt to use religion simply for political advantage, or to impress people of his piousness, contradicted the very character and integrity of Abraham Lincoln.

Schuyler Colfax, who would eventually become Vice-President of the United States, said Lincoln would often get up as early as four o'clock in the morning in order that he might have time to read his Bible and pray before visitors would begin to arrive at the White House. A book, *How Lincoln Prayed,* by William Johnstone, tells the story of a distinguished New York lawyer who went to the White House and asked for an hour interview:

"Mr. Lincoln said that the pressure of public duties forced him to decline such an interview. He urged that it was important. The President declined. The gentleman was leaving when Mr. Lin-

Replica of Lincoln's birthplace, Hodgenville, Kentucky

coln stopped him and asked if he would be willing to come at five o'clock the next morning. He gladly agreed to do so and arrived at the White House the next morning ...

"On consulting his watch at the street lamp he found he had made a mistake of an hour and that it was only four o'clock. He determined to walk about the grounds until the time agreed upon. Coming near a window of one of the rooms of the Presidential mansion, he heard sounds of apparent distress. On listening he found it was the voice of

(pgs. 122 & 123) Lincoln Memorial, Washington, D.C.

**'O, thou God who heard Solomon in the night . . .
I cannot guide the affairs of this nation without thy help.'**

A. Lincoln

The White House, Lincoln Administration

the President engaged in an agony of prayer. The burden of his petition was:

" 'O God, I cannot see my way. Give me light. I am ignorant, give me wisdom. Teach me what to do and help me to do it. Our country is in peril. O God, it is thy country; save it for Christ's sake.'

"Here the gentleman felt his position to be questionable, and passing on, he left the President with his God. On entering the White House he mentioned what he had heard to the usher, who informed him that the President spent the hour between four and five every morning in prayer."

A professor James Murdoch of Cincinnati, lecturer, elocutionist and actor who spent three weeks in the White House as a guest of Lincoln, tells of a similar incident.

"One night—it was just after the Battle of Bull Run—I was restless and could not sleep. I was repeating the part which I was to take in a public performance. The hour was past midnight—indeed, it was coming near the dawn—when I heard low tones proceeding from a private room near where the President slept. The door was partly open. I saw the President kneeling beside an open window. The light was turned low in the room. His back was toward me. For a moment I was silent, looking in amazement and wonder. Then he cried out in tones so pleading and sorrowful, that the astonished listener was transfixed:

" 'O, thou God who heard Solomon in the night when he prayed for wisdom, hear me. I cannot lead this people, I cannot guide the affairs of this nation without Thy help. I am poor and weak and sinful. O God, who didst hear Solomon when he cried for wisdom, hear me and save this nation.' "

WHEN LINCOLN BECAME PRESIdent he chose the New York Avenue Presbyterian Church as a regular place of worship. Lincoln said later: "I went there because I liked the pastor, Mr. Gurley, and because he preached the gospel and let politics alone. I get enough politics during the week."

It was here that the President, for a time, also attended the midweek prayer meeting. Writes William Gladstone: "Politicians, who could not get to him at the White House, learning that he went to prayer meeting, would stand at the door of the church, hoping to have a word with him as he went in or came out. To avoid this annoyance, it was arranged that Lincoln should go through a small passageway between the rear of the church and the next building, entering the church by a door which opened into the pastor's room. Lincoln would sit there alone in the dark. Presumably no one but the pastor and sexton knew he was there. The door into the prayer meeting room would be left slightly open, so that he could hear everything that went on in the prayer meeting."

A lady who was still a member of the church when Johnstone wrote his book (1930) told him that "her husband, then a boy, attended the prayer meetings. He often saw Lincoln's shadow or silhouette on the window, resting his elbow on the arm of the chair, and his head on his hand. He said it was the saddest picture he ever saw.

"Curious to know if the President returned to the White House, on two oc-casions when there was a light snow on the ground, he followed him, trying to step in Lincoln's steps. They were the biggest steps he ever tried to follow, and led direct to the White House."

Lincoln once told an intimate newspaper friend, Noah Brooks: "I have been driven many times upon my knees by the overwhelming conviction that I had nowhere else to go. My own wisdom, and that of all about me, seemed insufficient for that day."

During the Civil War Lincoln originated a gigantic plan called the Sanitary Commission—to care for the sick and wounded soldiers. It proved very successful. When Dr. John D. Hill, a prominent Buffalo physician and member of the commission, later complimented the President for conceiving such an idea, Lincoln replied:

"You must carry your thanks to a Higher Being. One stormy night I tossed on my bed, unable to sleep as I thought of the terrible sufferings of our soldiers and sailors. I spent an hour in agonizing prayer to God for some method of relief, and he put the Sanitary Commission in my mind, with all its details, as distinctly as though the instructions had been written out by pen and handed to me. Hereafter, always thank your heavenly Father, and not me, for this organization, which has eased so much pain and saved so many lives."

But perhaps one of the most striking stories of Lincoln and prayer—and one of the best documented—surrounds the Battle of Gettysburg.

In a Washington hospital Lincoln stood at the bedside of General Sickles, who had just had his leg amputated due to a wound at Gettysburg. Sickles asked

the President whether or not he had been anxious about the battle at Gettysburg. General James Rusling, who was also with the President, told of the conversation:

"'No, I was not; some of my Cabinet and many others in Washington were, but I had no fears.'

"General Sickles inquired how this was, and seemed curious about it. Mr. Lincoln hesitated, but finally replied:

"'Well, I will tell you how it was. In the pinch of the campaign up there, when everybody seemed panic-stricken, and nobody could tell what was going to happen, oppressed by the gravity of our affairs, I went to my room one day, and I locked the door, and got down on my knees before Almighty God, and prayed to Him mightily for victory at Gettysburg. I told Him that this was His war, and our cause His cause, but we couldn't stand another Fredericksburg or Chancellorsville.

"'And I then and there made a solemn vow to Almighty God, that if He would stand by our boys at Gettysburg, I would stand by Him. And after that (I don't know how it was, and I can't explain it), soon a sweet comfort crept into my soul that God Almighty had taken the whole business into His own hands and that things would go all right at Gettysburg.'"

The President had been praying for Vicksburg too, and he told Sickles that

he believed "our heavenly Father is going to give us victory there too."

Word had not yet reached him that Vicksburg also had fallen—just the day before!

Some might feel that Lincoln's spiritual vow on victory at Gettysburg sounds like he was bargaining with God. And did he keep his vow? If so, how? One source declares that when he went to Gettysburg and saw the graves of thousands of U.S. soldiers, he then and there consecrated himself to Jesus Christ. Mrs. Lincoln spoke of Gettysburg's profound effect upon her husband. Other sources believe he was about to make a public profession of faith at the time an assassin's bullet struck him down.

The debate on the particulars of Lincoln's faith will go on; yet no one disputes that long before Gettysburg, Lincoln fully realized and lived out the conviction that "the Most High ruleth in the kingdom of men" (Dan. 4:32). The same verse says that God "giveth it to whomsoever he will." If the "Almighty Ruler of Nations" at that time in history had put the reins of leadership into the hands of a man of lesser integrity than Lincoln, the Union might have never survived.

## CHAPTER EIGHT

# THE ERA OF D. L. MOODY

CHICAGO CAN NEVER ERASE the memory of the great disaster that befell her little more than one hundred years ago. On an October Sunday evening in 1871, ominous flames erupted on the city's south side. By midnight the entire populace was fleeing in panic as the inferno swept northward block by block, reducing the city to ashes.

When the city courthouse bell began to ring out the alarm and the first fire engines hurried toward the scene, a prominent Chicagoan named D. L. Moody was just concluding a regular Sunday evening evangelistic service in his tabernacle on the north side. Hearing the confusion outside, he and his soloist, Ira D. Sankey, promptly dismissed the capacity crowd. Hundreds in the gathering rushed to the aid of others or their own families.

As Moody made his way toward his own home, hurricane-like southwest winds from the fire blew sparks down around him, touching off first one house, then another. "The city's doomed," he said to his wife Emma as he walked in his front door.

The Moodys thought their own home perhaps far enough from the blaze to escape, but in the early morning hours police knocked and urged a getaway. The parents dispatched their two children to the suburbs with a neighbor and began gathering up a few of their belongings.

Among them was a cherished protrait of D. L. Moody by the most famous portrait artist of the day. "G. P. A. Healy" had given it to him upon Moody's return from a dramatically successful campaign in Great Britain where he had moved the hearts of more than a million people.

His wife urged him to save it.

"Take my own picture!" he laughed. "That would be a joke. Suppose I meet some friends in the same trouble as

**Out of the great Chicago fire
came the fires of revival.**

ourselves and they say, "Hullo Moody, glad you have escaped. What's that you've saved and cling to so affectionately?' Wouldn't it sound well to reply, 'Oh, I've got my own portrait!'"

Moody wouldn't touch it, but looters already on the scene obligingly cut it out of its frame and handed it to his wife.

It was not the character of Dwight L. Moody to glory in himself, but rather, to glory in what God could do for the man who put his trust in Jesus Christ.

The great Chicago fire destroyed Moody's home, his church and even the impressive Chicago YMCA he had launched, but in Moody's eyes it was not the worst catastrophe that could happen to man. Far worse that anyone should not hear clearly the gospel.

By the time of the Chicago fire Moody had already uplifted Jesus Christ to millions at home and abroad, but by the time of his death more than a quarter century later some would estimate his total audience as high as one hundred million. And the impact of a Chicago Bible institute he founded would resound around the world in the century to come.

Moody's spiritual life started in the back of a shoe store in Boston in 1855 when a dry-goods salesman named Edward Kimball, who also happened to be Moody's Sunday School teacher, led him to Jesus Christ.

Kimball afterward thought he had made a rather weak plea, but the next morning Moody "thought the old sun shone a good deal brighter than it ever had before—I thought that it was just smiling upon me; and as I walked out upon Boston Common and heard the birds singing in the trees, I thought they were all singing a song to me.

"Do you know," he later recalled, "I fell in love with the birds. I had never cared for them before. It seemed to me that I was in love with all creation. I had not a bitter feeling against any man, and I was ready to take all men to my heart."

Before long, Moody (who had little formal education) went west to Chicago and established himself as a first-rate shoe salesman. He invested in real es-

Moody rounding up children for his Sunday School.

tate and soon began to amass a small fortune. Moody could well have become a millionaire, said his close friends, but the Wall Street panic of 1857 convinced him he should not regard faith as primarily "an aid to fortune."

Meanwhile, Moody had also been rounding up street urchins from the poor section of Chicago's north side and before long his burgeoning mission Sunday school hosted hundreds weekly. Darting from one house or shanty to the next, he left others breathless in his dogged pursuit of prospects. At one point his class met in an old dance hall, another time in an abandoned freight car. Often he would ride around the streets on a pony, with an ample supply of maple sugar and apples to hand out as an encouragement for boys and girls to attend his class. The children loved him.

Daily Moody pressed almost everyone he met in Chicago with the question, "Are you a Christian?" One by one, men were converted.

The Sunday school work grew. Eventually Moody made a Chicago banker superintendent, then later his good friend John V. Farwell, at the time Chicago's wealthiest retail merchant (who would later be overtaken by Marshall Field). In 1860 President-elect Abraham Lincoln visited Moody's class. Before he left he told the young urchins, "I was once as poor as any boy in the school, but I am now President of the United States, and if you attend to

Abraham Lincoln visits Moody's Sunday School.

A New England scene in the 1860's, a decade when D. L. Moody was campaigning across America.

what is taught you here, some one of you may yet be President of the United States."

DURING THE CIVIL WAR Moody spent some of his time as a volunteer unordained chaplain in the front lines. In the frequent presence of death, he aided the wounded and urgently pressed men about their soul's eternal destiny. Moody, incidentally, never did become ordained, a decision which later worked to his advantage as he had opportunity to preach to millions across denominational lines.

Moody eventually gave up his flourishing shoe business and never again accepted a salary. Rather, he launched out on simple faith in every Christian venture he undertook. Time and again when funds were low or non-existent he saw God answer prayer. He rubbed shoulders frequently with millionaires, among them his good friend Cyrus McCormick, inventor of the combine harvester, who helped Moody establish the Chicago YMCA movement and gave liberally to it. (Later McCormick's son, Cyrus, Jr., would become one of the first trustees of the Moody Bible Institute.)

While at an international YMCA convention in Indianapolis in 1870 Moody was thrilled by the singing of a U. S. Government revenue worker from Pennsylvania named Ira Sankey. After hearing Sankey sing with great pathos, *There is a Fountain Filled with Blood*, Moody urged him to join the Chicago ministry. Sankey finally agreed, but on a trial basis. Thus originated the Moody-Sankey team that would later take both America and Great Britain by storm.

By the summer of '72 Chicago had begun to rise from the ashes, and a modest newly-built 1,400-seat Moody Tabernacle served as a center of relief and evangelism. Then Dwight L. Moody took off on a visit to Great Britain. Among Christians he met there was a wholesale butcher named Henry Varley, who one day remarked casually to Moody that "the world has yet to see what God will do with a man fully consecrated to Him."

Moody thought about those words for weeks, and decided one day that, by God's power, he would be that man.

Somewhat on the spur of the moment Moody was invited to speak in a London church. At the close he asked those who wanted "to have your lives changed by the power of God through faith in Jesus Christ as a personal Saviour" and who "wanted to become Christians" to rise. People rose everywhere. Moody thought they had misunderstood and tried to clarify his invitation. Scores came forward as Moody and the host minister looked on astonished. The phenomenon repeated itself the next night.

Moody returned to the States, now envisioning a British Isles campaign. He and Sankey laid plans, but somehow Moody faulted in his usual administrative efficiency and failed to communicate his intentions to his contacts in Great Britain.

When Moody and Sankey arrived at Liverpool in June, 1873, they found no one to meet them. Worse yet, Moody soon learned that all three of the prime contacts upon whom he had counted had died. So Moody asked a flustered friend in York to set up some evangelistic meetings in that city.

One morning as they waited for something to happen, Moody quipped to his associate, "I say, Sankey, here we are, a couple of white elephants!"

The ministers of York were suspicious. Americans? "Why do they want to come to York?" "What's the YMCA up to?" "Whoever heard of a mission in midsummer?"

Meetings did begin, however, in York's Corn Exchange. Little seemed to happen at first—at least on the surface. The British were not used to Moody's informal style of preaching, nor with Sankey's portable organ. They winced at the American evangelist's accent and his sometimes poor English, but the spirit of God began to work.

D. L. Moody sharply denounced sin, but also made clear to his audiences, many of Calvinistic bent, that God loves all men, even the worst of sinners. Listeners heard him blend the warmth and affection of Jesus as Friend with the awe and reverence of the Lord as God.

" 'To as many as received Him," he

would quote, "to them gave He power to become the sons of God'—*Him,* mark you! Not a dogma, not a creed, not a myth, but a *Person.*"

Sankey's music caught hold. Crowds grew. The campaign extended into weeks, then months—first Edinburgh, later Glasgow, finally London. Thousands were converted, homes were transformed, lives changed—genuinely, permanently—an impact that would be felt throughout England for decades. It started with England's middle class, later spread to the poor, and eventually permeated even the aristocracy, including the Princess of Wales. When the campaign closed no less than two years later, all Great Britain was talking about Moody and Sankey.

One Birmingham minister, who had prayed for revival but did not expect it

to come through two Americans, told Moody, "The work is most plainly of God, for I can see no relation between yourself and what you have done."

Moody laughed and replied, "I should be very sorry if it were otherwise."

Moody was not without opposition.

Some newspapers affirmed the campaign's impact on Great Britain. Other journalists scorched the evangelist, assumed unworthy financial motives and criticized Moody's English. Certain jealous clergy spread false rumors which Moody had to head off. But he had predicted such. "There will be many bitter things said, and many lies started," he assured, "and as someone has said, a lie will get half round the world before the truth gets its boots on!"

But in the city of London alone the Moody-Sankey campaign reached an estimated 1.5 million and, seven years later, Moody's preaching mission at England's erudite Cambridge University would touch off a spiritual revival that would ultimately send hundreds of students around the world as missionaries.

BACK HOME, AMERICA TOO needed Moody's message, perhaps as never before. The Civil War, like all wars, had disrupted general morality. People chased after easy wealth. Corruptions penetrated high

political office. Before launching a campaign in Philadelphia, Moody touched off a small revival at Princeton University. At Philadelphia one evening President Grant and several of his Cabinet sat on the platform. There was the New York campaign of 1876—and many more to follow in the cities and towns across America, spanning at least a quarter century until his death during a Kansas City campaign in 1899, just a few days before the turn of the Twentieth Century.

Many contend that Dwight L. Moody left his greatest legacy in 1886 when he established the Moody Bible Institute of Chicago.

The evangelist conceived the institution as a school to train Christian workers to reach Chicago. Moody called some of his friends to Chicago's Pacific Hotel in early 1887—among them Farwell, Cyrus McCormick Jr. and lumber king T. W. Harvey—and founded the Chicago Evangelization Society.

But from China came a letter from C. T. Studd, Great Britain's famed athlete who had gone to China as a missionary following the Moody-sparked revival at Cambridge University. Studd had just inherited a part of his father's fortune (his famous sportsman father had also been converted under Moody). Studd enclosed $50,000 to start a gospel work in north India, where the fortune had

Moody in London, England.     (pgs. 138 & 139) Dwight L. Moody preaches to capacity crowd

Buildings of the Moody Bible Institute, Chicago

been made.

Moody could not honor that precise request but wrote Studd that he would do the next best thing and open a Training School with it, "from which men and women will go to all parts of the world to evangelize."

Soon afterward Moody spotted a lot next to his base of operations at Chicago Avenue and Wells and prayed that the Lord might provide that land for a school. In time God did, and also several other adjacent lots. Dormitories went up to house 200 men and 50 women. He named as its first superintendent Reuben A. Torrey, a Greek and Hebrew scholar who, although he had sat under "higher critics" in Germany, "returned wholeheartedly to believe in the Bible, the whole Bible, as the Word of God ..."

Moody also saw the need for religious books and established the Moody Colportage Association. He conceived the low-cost religious paperback for the masses at least a half century before the modern-day paperback came into its own.

Little could Moody have foreseen the tremendous and far-reaching impact the Moody Bible Institute would have in the Twentieth Century ... a vast, multi-faceted world ministry that is still rapidly expanding. The school, currently attended by 1300 students, has turned out nearly four thousand career

missionaries (including 21 martyrs). It
has fed into the pulpits and churches of
America thousands of pastors, musi-
cians and Christian educators and has
sent thousands of other graduates into
all kinds of evangelical movements and
institutions.

It has pioneered in religious radio,
with Chicago's WMBI following
promptly on the heels of America's first
radio station—KDKA, Pittsburgh.
(Moody Bible Institute today also owns
stations in Cleveland, Moline (Ill.),
Chattanooga and Spokane) and produces programs for more than 250
other stations.

Since 1940 its missionary aviation
program (now based in Tennessee and
considered tops in its field) has trained
some 70 percent of the world's missionary pilots. Its publishing house,
Moody Press, turns out more than 100
book titles a year, and *Moody Monthly,*
the nation's fastest-growing Christian
magazine, has a paid circulation in ex-
cess of one quarter million.

The California-based Moody Institute of Science produces films that
reach into churches, mission fields,
military bases, public schools and industry, and are viewed by one half million persons a day. An evening school

enrolls more than 1,000 and a correspondence school more than 90,000.

It seems that wherever D. L. Moody went, he set in motion, under God's power and wisdom, spiritual events that would eventually touch the ends of the earth.

"Some day you will read in the papers," the evangelist once said, "that Moody is dead. Don't you believe a word of it. At that moment I shall be more alive than I am now ... I was born of the flesh in 1837, I was born of the Spirit in 1855. That which is born of the flesh may die. That which is born of the Spirit shall live forever."

IN THE NINETEENTH CENTURY God raised up at least two other great evangelists on the American scene.

In 1830 Charles G. Finney preached for six months at Rochester, New York, and saw one hundred thousand souls make profession of faith in Jesus Christ. It is estimated that the preaching of Finney, who founded Oberlin (Ohio) College and served as its first president, influenced change in one half million lives.

Finney did not inherit his religious

Left: Moody Church, Chicago, founded by D. L. Moody. Top: The Moody Bible Institute concert band. Right: inner plaza of the campus. Below: one of the offices within the Chicago complex, which employs some six hundred.

bent. In his home he never heard the name of God, except in blasphemy. Though reared in the backwoods of western New York state, he emerged to study law and pursue in Adams, New York, what promised to be a brilliant legal career. Since Finney's law books contained many references to the Bible, he bought one for reference, but he always made sure it was hid under other volumes when anyone else was around.

Finney visited the Presbyterian church in town and found the congregation praying for revival. The young

lawyer offered only scorn and ridicule until young people in the church, led by the girl Finney would eventually marry, began to pray for him. The Spirit began to convict of sin. Finney could not eat or sleep. Finally one evening he fled to woods on the edge of town, poured out his sins to God and found great release.

He raced back into town to shout out the news of his salvation—in offices, in homes, on the street. Within twenty-four hours he had won twenty-four to the Lord, among them another lawyer and a distiller.

Finney dropped law and began to plead the cause of Jesus Christ. He launched into evangelism and took onto his team a man named Nash, who made prayer his sole and all-consuming role. When Finney preached, Nash stayed behind and prayed. Wherever Finney conducted campaigns—in London, New York, or elsewhere—thousands responded. In Boston, stronghold of Unitarianism, fifty thousand accepted the Lord in just one week.

When Finney preached in Philadelphia, "a number of lumberjacks who had floated their logs down the river took in the meeting. Many were converted, and on returning to their work eighty miles upstream, they took the story of salvation with them. At home they organized prayer circles, held family devotions, conducted simple services, and on returning within a year's time, they asked for a minister, saying that five thousand had been saved during the year—without a preacher!"

"What will you do with Jesus Christ?" Finney always demanded a verdict on this all-important issue. Many of those converted went on to

Billy Sunday

exert a profound social impact in their day. Finney continued as educator and evangelist until his death in 1875, the year D. L. Moody returned from his two-year campaign in Great Britain.

FLASH NOW TO a few decades after Finney's death and observe the impact of a one-time major league ball player named Billy Sunday, who played with the then Chicago White Stockings. Fans labeled him the only man who could round the diamond touching every base in fourteen seconds. Billy

Sunday received Christ at the Pacific Garden Mission in Chicago around the time Dwight L. founded Moody Bible Institute two miles away.

Sunday continued in pro ball four more years, until resigning for full-time evangelism. His great physical stamina as a ball player carried over well into his new career, during which he would preach twenty thousand times! In 1917 in New York a million and a half people heard Sunday during a ten-week campaign. Some two million people, it is said, gave their hearts to God during the Sunday campaigns, which spanned a quarter century.

Sunday would roll up his sleeves and deliver his sermons machine-gun style, roaming vigorously about the platform. No one denied his color and showmanship, but there was much more—the historic gospel that transformed the lives of millions.

And it is here, perhaps, that the record needs to be set straight. God takes mere men and uses them, together with the Scriptures and the unseen power of the Holy Spirit, to bring men and women, boys and girls, to Himself. Genuine conversion is impossible apart from the supernatural. Men can manipulate the counterfeit, but real salvation is of God.

Three men out of the Nineteenth Century helped set great spiritual forces in motion. There were millions across America whose lives, whose homes, whose careers, were salvaged, redirected, transformed, as a direct result. The majority ultimately reached may never have even heard Moody, or Finney, or Sunday. But they heard the gospel from someone "down the line," many steps removed, who cared enough to "pass it on." Christians often multiply. One genuine conversion can have far-reaching impact.

Had not God singled out a handful of individuals in each century who could help reverse the inevitable degeneracy in the hearts of men, America even by now may have died.

CHAPTER NINE

# THE EVANGELICAL
# FACE OF AMERICA

I N THE WASHINGTON HILTON one morning in early February, 1974, under the thickening cloud of Watergate, Iowa Senator Harold Hughes stood to address a National Prayer Breakfast. The president, vice-president, chief justice and other top-echelon figures sat at the head table. Below were gathered some 2,500 guests—senators, congressmen, judges, members of the Cabinet and many others from the higher ranks of government, business and various fields.

The 6′3″, 250-pound Hughes, a former truck-driver, moved promptly into telling of his deliverance from alcoholism. "I was beaten to my knees in despair," he said. "I cried out to God, and from that moment my life changed." Then, "thundering like an Old Testament prophet," according to one description, he declared that America "has wallowed in luxury and dirtied its nest." He called for repen-

tance, assuring that God could use men's "indiscretions" to "build up His people."

"The Word of God came in Jesus Christ and revealed eternal life," Hughes assured. "The debt has been paid in the blood of our Savior."

In their book, *WASHINGTON: Christians in the Corridors of Power,* Journalists Jim Hefley and Ed Plowman describe the scene that followed:

"At the end he (Hughes) asked everyone to join hands around tables and pray audibly for renewal and whatever came to mind as a need. The distinguished individuals glanced uneasily at one another, then one by one people began extending hands to each other. Only those at the head table refrained.

"For a moment there was silence, then a voice here and another there began to pray, then others, and soon there was a crescendo of voices simultaneously thanking God and imploring

Senator Harold Hughes:
"The debt has been paid
in the blood of the Savior".

Him for help in personal and national life. Finally, Hughes spoke a closing prayer into the microphone, and the crowd quieted. When he sat down no one stirred, no clicking of cups marred the hush. Then in the stillness someone began applauding and as one the great body arose and accorded Hughes a long ovation."

Hughes has established himself as an unashamed Christian and a forceful voice for spiritual renewal in Washington and across the land. But, encouragingly, many others with whom he rubs shoulders seem to echo his convictions. The National Prayer Breakfast, held every February just before Groundhog Day, "may be well timed," write Hefley and Plowman, for, "like the proverbial groundhog, some politicians come out for God only once a year." But much genuine spiritual resurgence seems to lie behind the surface.

Some twenty percent of U.S. Senators and another fifty representatives now meet in weekly prayer groups. Numerous figures in key government positions speak winsomely of their personal faith in Jesus Christ, and are winning others. At least seventeen groups meet weekly in the Pentagon for prayer and Bible study, and scores more exist throughout almost all the major government agencies.

It has not always been so, despite the

## Look almost every direction today, and you will find an evangelical renaissance.

nation's rich evangelical heritage. Most of the Twentieth Century, until more recently, had been somewhat of a spiritual "dry spell," perhaps due in part to two world wars and the inroads of a theological liberalism which had undermined many pulpits of the land. Oh, the real Christians were around, to be sure. But somehow no great number of the real opinion makers who were shaping the course of historical events took notice.

The climate now is a far cry from the one, say, in the 30's, when the liberal churchmen and those they influenced seemingly held sway. At that time few in the ranks of leadership anywhere listened very seriously to those who propounded an orthodox Christian doctrine. In a 1974 Boston address, U.S. Rep. John B. Anderson of Illinois, an evangelical, vividly described the contrast between then and now:

At that time, he says, "it was *they* (the liberals) who denied the supernatural acts of God, conforming the gospel to the canons of modern science. It was *they* who advocated laws and legislation as the modern substitutionary atonement for the sins of mankind.... *They* were the "beautiful people," and *we*—you will recall—were the "kooks." We were regarded as rural, reactionary, illiterate fundamentalists who just didn't know better.

"Well, things have changed. Now *they* are the "kooks"—and *we* are the "beautiful people." *Our* churches are growing, and theirs are withering.... *They* are tired, worn-out 19th century liberals trying to repair the pieces of an optimism shattered by world wars, race riots, population explosion, and the spectre of worldwide famine."

LOOK ALMOST EVERY DIRECTION today and you will find an evangelical "renaissance." What is the evidence?

The churches of a nation stand as the backbone of its spiritual life and provide one barometer by which to measure its spiritual temperature. Where is the action today? In the evangelical churches. Many are thriving, growing, reaching out into their communities with vigor and vision. They may not all agree on methods. But collectively they are making an impact on the nation at its grassroots.

More evidence:

• The public press which, little more than a decade or two ago, simply ignored or ridiculed anything that smacked of fundamentalism, lavishly ballyhooed the "Jesus movement," and today it generally treats evangelical Christians with fairness and respect.

• Evangelical book sales have flourished in the past few years, some books becoming national best sellers. Super-markets and big-name chain

**Some twenty percent of U.S. Senators and another fifty representatives now meet in weekly prayer groups.**

stores display and sell evangelical books and an average of two new Christian bookstores open every day.

- *U.S. News and World Report,* among other observers, cites a "Boom in Protestant Schools," most of them evangelical.

- Thousands of neighborhood Bible study groups have sprung up across the land.

- A vigorous "Jews for Jesus" movement (some prefer "Hebrew Christian") has surfaced, as more and more Jewish folk tell of having discovered Jesus as their Messiah.

- Professional athletes by the score have become Christians and "pass it on" through weekly chapel sessions.

- Millions of Americans simultaneously watch a single evangelistic crusade on television.

- Student Christian movements flourish on the secular university campus, attracting thousands.

- A son of the United States President experienced conversion and now studies at an evangelical school.

- Businessmen and office workers hold lunch-hour Bible breaks.

- A vigorous Christian thrust suddenly has emerged among airline workers—pilots, stewardesses, ground crews.

- Several figures in the Watergate scandal have found Jesus Christ as Savior.

**Look almost every direction today, and you will find an evangelical renaissance.**

• An astronaut returned from the moon has gone into full-time evangelism.

• While once-prominent liberal seminaries close or struggle to stay alive with a handful of students, two evangelical seminaries in Texas alone have enrolled a combined total of almost four thousand.

And the momentum continues. Many look on amazed, or at least perplexed.

Let us not forget, however, that over the years, faithful Christians have laid the foundations for the evangelical renaissance, however quietly. "One generation shall praise thy works to another" (Ps. 145:4), says the Scriptures, and we must give credit to all faithful predecessors. The evangelical threads of American history still hold, because God has seen to it. "Jesus Christ is the same yesterday, today and forever" (Heb. 13:8).

THE DRIFT OF THE IVY LEAGUE schools—one by one—from their Christian foundations, repeated itself again and again as both lower and higher education in America went secular. No longer was Jesus Christ the focal point of learning and knowledge, nor were subjects taught from a distinctly Christian point of view.

But in this century many Bible institutes and Christian colleges have emerged to do, in a sense, what the Ivy League started out to do. Meanwhile, at the elementary level, tens of thousands of U.S. youngsters, confirms an article in *U.S. News and World Report,* are shifting from public into private classrooms—most of these schools evangelical.

And there's much more behind it than the race or busing issues, says the report. Parents are looking for discipline, a better learning environment, a religious emphasis. They also want, says an official for the National Association of Christian Schools, "a total education—where Christ is in the classroom."

No education can be complete, they say, where the Lord of the Universe, "in whom are hid all the treasures of wisdom and knowledge," is shoved aside. The God of history is also the God of science, or of whatever the subject may be.

A growing force of Christian professors in our secular colleges and universities are making this same point—and they're beginning to be noticed—in a broad range of fields from physics, sociology and mathematics to the language arts, economics and biology. One sacred cow that has come under fire is Darwin's theory of evolution. John N. Moore, professor of natural science at Michigan State University, is typical of this new breed. Once an evolutionist,

The evangelical thrust today has great vigor at many levels. Left: United Airlines pilot Bob Burdick helped launch Christian movement among airline workers. Top: a San Gabriel classroom scene in the fast-growing California Association of Christian Schools. Above: a converted convict shares his story. Right: A young Barrington, Illinois, couple tell of changed lives.

**Could God be raising up
a young generation of Christians
who will saturate America
with the gospel in
the years ahead?**

The Regeneration Singers

he has made a full turn and now points his students toward the Creator to explain the origins of the universe, life and man. "Reputable scientists in each decade since Darwin's book was published have been critical of evolution," says Moore. "Why didn't my teachers inform me of that when I was an undergraduate?"

Vigorous evangelical movements in many universities have also forced many secularists to take another look. Student evangelists like Campus Crusade's Josh McDowell, who draws thousands wherever he goes, combine scholarship with head-on evangelism. When he comes with his book, *Evidence That Demands a Verdict* (an impressive

volume of apologetics for the Christian faith), professors often rush to acquire the book so they can be better prepared for the challenge they know they'll have to face from Christians in the classroom.

On the campus and off, the gospel and evangelism are far more visible than they were a quarter century ago. The massive ministry of Billy Graham and some believe that the other parachurch agencies have helped create a much more receptive climate for all who preach the fundamental gospel. Meanwhile, some churches—are busing literally thousands into their Sunday schools each week. Some caution that quantity does not always necessarily

This fleet of vans at a San Jose church reflects today's vigorous bus evangelism, especially by Bible Baptists.

mean quality, but there is no question that God is very much at work through many agencies in these exciting times.

The current Christian surge notwithstanding, what about the negatives: crime, drugs, falling moral standards, corruption in government, and hedonism—the drive to achieve "life with gusto" at any price?

We have them all, to be sure. Yet it is against this very backdrop that the gospel seems to be flourishing. For Jesus Christ alone satisfies the deepest longings of men's souls.

The Jesus movement in part grew out of a youth culture that first rejected the materialistic lifestyle of many adults, then turned to drugs and rejected that also. Real happiness has evaded most Americans of all ages, and this may provide fertile soil for the gospel as the nation moves from its bicentennial into a new era.

In a recent seven page report, *U.S. News and World Report,* called the "Pursuit of Happiness," an "elusive goal in affluent America." On the surface, it said, the well being of Americans seems to go beyond anything the nation's founders might have foreseen in 1776 while proclaiming the pursuit of happiness to be an "unalienable right."

While "some Americans ... are returning to strongly held religious beliefs," said the article, "large numbers of ordinary people are locked into emptiness."

The report alluded to "The authority of religious belief that once enabled God-fearing Americans to cope with adversity and loneliness, in life or in death." It concluded by quoting English philosopher John Stuart Mill: "Those only are happy ... who have their minds fixed on some object other than their own happiness; on the happiness of others, on the improvement of mankind, even on some art of pursuit, followed not as a means, but as itself an ideal end. Aiming thus at something else, they find happiness by the way."

If a national news magazine can make the pursuit of happiness a cover story and attempt an interpretation, however short it may have fallen, surely the climate of America is ripe for Christians to show others where true happiness can be found. Millions are willing to at least listen.

WHAT, THEN, WILL IT TAKE to convince the pursuers of happiness that Christians really have some-

Harry Saulnier (right), founder of Chicago's historic Pacific Garden Mission (below), is among those many who believe that social reform at its best starts with the gospel of Jesus Christ.

thing to offer? A joy that is genuine and contagious—even in adversity (the Scriptures speak much about joy). The Holy Spirit within—given full freedom. Unashamedly lifting up Jesus Christ, who said, "I am come that ye might have life, and that ye might have it more abundantly" (John 10:10).

While some Christians may find it fairly easy to market happiness to this generation, they may not find it quite so easy to confront people with the reality of sin.

Yet the two are obviously interrelated. Even Dr. Karl Menninger, world-renowned psychiatrist, has stepped forth with a book called *Whatever Became of Sin?*

For years most psychiatrists and psychologists have dismissed "sin" as irrelevant. They have accused religion of "producing guilt" and have counseled patients to cast off their guilt feelings and do what they want.

But Menninger believes mental health and moral health are identical

Millions of Americans have found Jesus Christ as the answer. Left: Jimmy Dorsey, who wrote the hymn, "Precious Lord, Take My Hand." Top center, Rita Warren, a Hebrew Christian. Top right, John Moore, Michigan State science professor, who sees the dogma of evolution crumbling. Lower right: James Johnson, assistant secretary of the Navy, testifies of his faith.

and the only way our suffering, struggling, anxious society can hope to prevent mental ills is by recognizing the reality of sin.

When asked in a *Chicago Daily News* interview how this should be done, he answered, "Preach! Tell it like it is. Say it from the pulpits. Cry it from the housetops!

"If the concept of personal responsibility and answerability for ourselves and for others were to return to common acceptance," he says, "and man once again would feel guilt for sins and repent and establish a conscience that would act as a deterrent for further sin, then hope would return to the world."

These words did not come from an evangelist.

Perhaps America's moral conscience is stronger than we think, and a growing chorus of voices—even from outside the fold—is shouting that things have gone far enough.

When *The Saturday Evening Post,* defunct for some time, announced it was making a comeback, its letter to prospective subscribers read:

"A great joy is spreading across the country—and it's about time. The big trend (despite what certain politicians say) is back to family life, a reunification of our nation, dedication to hard work and thrift, public decency instead of public immorality."

The *Post* said its magazine would be welcomed into homes as truly American literature, safe for the youngest youngster to read, full of vitality for all the young in heart, for imaginative folks who remember what life was like before there were riots, tight dollars, terrible trash."

This may be little more than good sales copy with a touch of nostalgia. But the fact that the *Post* thinks it can succeed with this formula suggests it sees a genuine vacuum into which it can move. And it is exactly this vacuum into which Christians can move in the immediate years ahead.

If the Lord tarries in His return, can America truly be evangelized in this generation?

Ben Wattenberg, America's foremost demographic expert, points out some striking factors that may be significant:

The U.S. birth rate peaked in 1957 at 3.7 children per home. By mid-1973 it had plunged to 1.7! As a result, America's population projection for the next generation has been revised downward by some fifty million people.

At the same time, the wave from the baby boom in the fifties has moved into high school and college (most of those born at the 1957 peak are now high school seniors).

It is this generation and those a little older that has proved so responsive to the gospel—especially in the last five years. Generally, they are able to articulate the gospel much better than their parents could at their same age, perhaps due in part to the vigorous para-church movements who have *shown them* how to do so.

Could God be raising up a generation of young Christians (on the wave of the baby boom) who will saturate America with the gospel in the next few years— in an America with fifty million fewer people to evangelize? The ratio of Christians per capita, at least, would seem to be improving. Or, instead, will God break into the American scene in a less predictable and more dramatic way—as in the revivals of the past?

Does this ignore the evil around us? No, but it sets it in perspective. Evil may continue to wax worse, but the gospel will go forth. The wheat and the tares will grow together, and as the two polarize, perhaps true Christians will shine ever brighter against the darkening backdrop.

## CHAPTER TEN

# WHO IS UNDERMINING OUR REPUBLIC?

S INCE THE UNITED STATES SUP-
reme COURT announced its now
famous "regent's Prayer" decision in
June, 1962, effects have resounded across the land. Over the past decade and
a half scores of other cases, in the wake
of the Supreme Court's original move,
have come before the courts. Plaintiffs
have cited everything from classroom
devotions and prayer at school milk
break to baccalaureate services and
even the Pledge of Allegiance itself as
"unconstitutional."

Meanwhile, some public school
superintendents and principals, who
fear local lawsuits, regarded the issue a
"hot potato" and hastened to silence all
mention of God in the classroom. One
grade school principal told his teachers,
"when you're in the classroom, you
have no religion."

When man circled the moon for the
first time just four days before Christmas, 1968, millions around the world

watched and listened as astronaut Frank
Borman read from the creation account
in the opening chapter of Genesis, "In
the beginning God ..." Infuriated
atheist Madalyn Mrray O'Hair has been
trying ever since to secure an official
government "censure."

At the crux of the crisis, of course, is
the First Amendment to the U. S. Constitution, which states that "Congress
shall make no law respecting an establishment of religion or prohibiting the
free exercise thereof."

Theologians have wrestled with this
passage of sixteen words. Historians
have explained it, lawyers have interpreted it, all with different viewpoints.
While admittedly the issues are complex, certain basics seem to be clear
when one examines the intent of the
founding fathers.

What was George Washington's attitude, for instance? Certainly not that
God should be left out of the affairs of

men. In his First Inaugural Address he declared:

"No people can be bound to acknowledge and adore the invisible hand which conducts the affairs of men more than the people of the United States. Every step by which they have advanced to the character of an independent nation seems to have been distinguished by some token of providential agency."

His Farewell Address, says historian Gaustad, even more persuasively extolled religion as the ground from which morality takes its rise, warning that "reason and experience both forbid us to expect that national morality can prevail in exclusion of religious principle."

Or consider the attitude of Benjamin Franklin at the very convention which ratified the U. S. Constitution.

The Constitutional Convention had begun its sessions on May 25, 1787, in the State House in Philadelphia. But it was getting nowhere. The weather was warm; tempers flared. On June 28, Benjamin Franklin rose. After lamenting the lack of progress after more than four weeks in session, Franklin declared to the gathering:

"I have lived, Sir, a long time; and the longer I live the more convincing Proofs I see of this Truth, That God governs in the Affairs of Men!—And if a Sparrow cannot fall to the Ground without his Notice, is it probable that an Empire can rise without his Aid?—We have been assured, Sir, in the Sacred Writings, that 'except the Lord build the House, they labor in vain that build it.' I firmly believe this;—and I also believe that without his concurring Aid we shall succeed in this political Building no better than the Builders of Babel: we shall be divided by our little partial local Interests, our Projects will be confounded and we ourselves shall become a Reproach and a Byeword down to future Ages. And what is worse, Mankind may hereafter, from this unfortunate

## National Morality demands religious principles

George Washington:
National morality demands religious principles

Instance, despair of establishing Government by human Wisdom, and leave it to Chance, War & Conquest.

"I therefore beg leave to move, That henceforth Prayers, imploring the Assistance of Heaven, and its Blessing on our Deliberations, be held in this Assembly every Morning before we proceed to Business ..."

This was the very Convention that passed the "establishment of religion" clause! Moreover, though both Washington and Franklin had a keen sense of divine providence, they were not evangelical Christians. Like a number of the founding fathers, they were essentially "deists" whose theologies and philosophies had been influenced by the rationalism that was rampant at that time. Therefore, their actions could hardly stem from an evangelical bias—though they respected those even among their own colleagues who held such convictions.

CONSIDER STILL ANOTHER INCIdent that hardly depicts our foundational legislators running from prayer and the Bible.

The American Revolution was in full swing. The Bible, through more than one hundred fifty years of early settlement in America, remained the base of her peoples' religious devotion, her education, her colonial government. These Bibles had been shipped in from England. Now, suddenly the American Revolution cut off this supply, and the stock dwindled.

Here was America in its greatest crisis yet— and without Bibles! Patrick Allison, Chaplain of Congress, placed before that body in 1777 a petition praying for immediate relief. It was assigned to a special committee which weighed the matter with great care, and reported:

"...that the use of the Bible is so universal and its importance so great that your committee refer the above to the consideration of Congress, and if Con-

**Theologians have wrestled with it, historians have explained it, lawyers have interpreted it— with different shades of viewpoint.**

gress shall not think it expedient to order the importation of types and paper, the Committee recommend that Congress will order the Committee of Congress to import 20,000 Bibles from Holland, Scotland, or elsewhere, into the different parts of the States of the Union.

"Whereupon it was resolved accordingly to direct said Committee to import 20,000 copies of the Bible."

During the session in the fall of 1780 the need arose once more.

Robert Aitken, who had set up in Philadelphia as a bookseller and publisher of *The Pennsylvania Magazine,* saw the need and set about quietly to do something about it. In early 1781 he petitioned Congress and received from them a green light to print the Bibles needed. The Book came off the press late the next year, and Congress approved it. So originated the "Bible of the Revolution," now one of the world's rarest books—the first American printing.

SOME HAVE OPPOSED Bible reading and prayer in the public schools under the sincere conviction that such practices are little more than ritual and tend to blunt rather than nourish a true spiritual experience. Some see it as possibly an infringement on the First Amendment. But others have simply been taken in by the secular philosophy of our time.

Has our Constitution really been transgressed, as some say?

At the time of the Constitution's adoption in 1787 the theocratic concept of government (rule by officials regarded as divinely guided) of the early Puritans had already given way to the concept of democracy (rule by the people). This called for separation of church and state. At the start of the Revolutionary War, for instance, Congregationalism was the established religion in three of the New England colonies; Massachusetts, Connecticut and New Hampshire. Six other colonies officially recognized the Anglican church.

In the years immediately after the war these colonies, one by one, disestablished their state religions. The fight for religious liberty, spearheaded by Thomas Jefferson, James Madison and many of the churches themselves, climaxed with the passing of the Virginia constitution in 1785. Shortly afterwards, this principle was to become a part of the fundamental law of the land.

Thus when these early statesmen framed the First Amendment to the Constitution, they were trying to guard against one thing, the establishment of a state church. This meant any church that might attempt to tie itself to the government or seek special privileges though it. While this amendment was originally directed only against Con-

162

We the People

*of the United States, in Order to form a more perfect Union, establish Justice, insure domestic Tranquility, provide for the common Defence, promote the general Welfare, and secure the Blessings of Liberty to ourselves and our Posterity, do ordain and establish this CONSTITUTION for the United States of America.*

Article I.

Ben Franklin

gress, in recent decades it has come to be regarded as applicable also to state legislation by virtue of the Fourteenth Amendment's "due process" clause.

Thus the men who wrote the Constitution forbade sectarianism in government. But they in no way suggested that God could be ignored in the governmental affairs of men. In fact, they assumed the very opposite—that God is above any human government— and this assumption was so unanimous it was not even debated!

The conviction that government is responsible to God, even in a democracy, permeates many of the documents of our nation. It explains also why all fifty of our state constitutions, patterned in part after the federal constitution, acknowledge God.

Not all our early leaders were necessarily fundamental in theology. But they sensed God's sovereign hand in human affairs, and they believed that "except the Lord build the house, they labour in vain that build it" (Ps. 127:1).

Times have changed, of course, for our society today is a pluralistic one as never before, the tide of secularism has swept away many of our spiritual values, and tolerance has been misconstrued to mean the minority can manipulate the majority. The problems of church-state separation we face today admittedly are complex and not easily solved. None of this, however,

changes the United States Constitution nor the intent of those who wrote it.

Who, then, is really undermining the Constitution? Certainly not those who wish to retain that spirit behind its inception—that God is supreme and that our democracy must stand on this assumption.

Furthermore, a society prospers not only when there is outward order imposed by law, but when there is inward order in the lives of its people. The founding fathers agreed unanimously that democracy, with all its inherent freedoms, could not thrive without a strong moral base. The Bible and the gospel have exerted a tremendous moral force upon the people of America, even among those who do not claim a personal Savior. Discourage this influence, and you immediately encourage a collapse of order in our democracy. It is not hard to spot signs of this collapse in many arenas today.

The Greeks, in fact, established the world's first democracy in the city-state of Athens. Citizens gathered in assembly to make their own laws. But the experiment failed because the Athenians lacked moral character.

France in the 18th century enjoyed some, if not all, of the freedoms guaranteed in our Bill of Rights. But their adventure in democracy, too, was short lived. Why? Largely because antireligions rationalists, disciples of Voltaire and Rousseau, undercut the spiritual and moral foundations of the land.

Back in 1851 Daniel Webster warned, "Let the religious element in man's nature be neglected, let him be influenced by no higher motives than low self-interest, and subjected to no stronger restraint than the limits of civil authority, and he becomes the creature of selfish passion or blind fanaticism."

Charles Malik, one-time Ambassador to the United States from Lebanon, has said, "The good (in the United States) would never have come into being without the blessing and the power of Jesus Christ."

Even Justice William O. Douglas, one not known for championing traditional Christian beliefs, declared in 1952 in the case of Zorach vs. Clauson: "We are a religious people and our institutions presuppose a Supreme Being."

This basic assumption, coupled with principles that have their roots in Scripture, lie at the base of our American democracy. These convictions also undergird our freedoms. Journalist and TV commentator Rus Walton, in his book *One Nation Under God*, observes that "to some freedom is a no-holds-barred opportunity for the big rip-off and the easy ride." Sooner or later freedom goes out the window, he says, if "the laws of men are not in harmony with the laws of God."

The third stanza of *America, the Beautiful* links the two concepts precisely:

> America! America! God mend thine
> every flaw,
> Confirm thy soul in self control, Thy
> liberty in law!

Would not the real danger then lie in the movement afoot today which is chipping away at the spiritual timbers built into the framework of our nation? Would it not lie with those who are waving piously the "establishment of

Independence Hall

religion" clause, while glossing over the second part of that same amendment they allege to defend? For that amendment not only rules against the establishment of religion, but also against "prohibiting the free exercise thereof."

Are not these the ones who are undermining the Constitution?

IF THE FOUNDATIONS of our Republic have indeed been eroded by stifling the spiritual base of our democracy, it is not the same spirit that prevailed among many of our early leaders. They worried not so much about the dangers of civil religion as they did about the erosion of our moral base. A loose link, at least, between patriotism and the Scriptures emerged in such movements as the American Bible Society, the American Tract Society and, especially, the American Sunday School Union (note the "American" emphasis in all three).

Even more significant, many statesmen who helped shape early America involved themselves heavily in these movements.

Take for instance the American Bible Society, founded in 1816 to distribute Bibles on a mass basis to the people of the land. One of its vice presidents was John Jay, also a former president of the Continental Congress and the first chief justice of the United States. DeWitt Clinton was elected governor of New

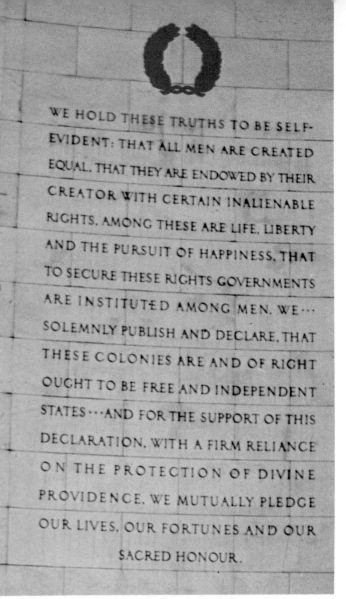

Jefferson Memorial

York while manager of the Society.

In its early decades the Society literally followed the wagon trains west, and provided God's Word for increasing numbers of immigrants in their own languages. It furnished Bibles to clamoring ministers, struggling Sunday schools and needy families in the wilderness.

The Society had its origins on horseback at the outset of the War of 1812, when missionaries Samuel J. Mills and J. M. Schermerhorn set out to explore the spiritual needs of the wilderness. They rode from Massachusetts to Nashville, there joined General Andrew Jackson and 1,500 soldiers on a steamer down to Natchez, Mississippi, then booked passage on a flatboat to New Orleans. It took them one month on horseback to push back up through the heavy forests and bridgeless rivers to Nashville. From there they rode on to Pittsburgh. Everywhere along the route they saw thousands of people with no Bibles for themselves or their children, and with little or no opportunity to hear any preaching. Out of this need came the ABS.

In 1820 the Society began to distribute Bibles to the Armed Services, a ministry which continues to this day. By 1870 the Society had several thousand auxiliaries across the country, and tens of thousands of unpaid Bible distributors.

Prominent early educators backed the movement and served on its board—among them Henry Rutgers, principal benefactor of the university that bears his name, and General Stephen Van Rensselaer, founder of the Rensselaer Polytechnic Institute. General Stonewall Jackson, long a warm friend of the Society, sometimes went from house to house to collect money himself for the support of its work.

In this century the Society has also moved into the gigantic task of Bible translation, providing Bibles not just for those on home soil, but for the nations of the world.

Francis Scott Key

Also, prominent government, business and religious leaders who saw the need of evangelistic literature, met in New York on May 11, 1825, to organize the American Tract Society. Over the years its membership roll included six U. S. presidents. By 1895 the operation had grown so large that a 23-story building was erected, one of New York's first skyscrapers (ATS moved to Oradell, New Jersey in 1962).

But perhaps no movement undergirded its evangelism with the spirit of patriotism as did the American Sunday School Union. The Sunday school movement had originated in England with Robert Raikes and was transplanted to America by another Englishman, Robert May. It took root with special vigor around Philadelphia, and out of that city in 1824 came a national movement, called the American Sunday School Union. In the next century and a half it planted thousands of Sunday schools across America, following the migration west from the Appalachian cabins to the frontier towns and the isolated hovels of the western Indian. Churches eventually sprang up from the majority of these Sunday schools—more than three thousand of them in this century alone. Though historically rural, its work today also penetrates the inner city.

The American Sunday School Un-

ion's link to great past patriots is easy to document.

Its prime mover was Dr. Benjamin Rush, signer of the Declaration of Independence and the most eminent American physician of his generation.

Among its original vice presidents was Bushrod Washington, nephew of George Washington. The American Sunday School Union originated probably the most widely circulated book ever written on George Washington.

Also among its early officers was John Marshall, one of the great chief justices of the United States Supreme Court.

Another long-time vice president was Pennsylvania Governor John Pollock, who, incidentally, introduced to America from Canada the gospel song, *I Love to Tell the Story,* and who, as director of the United States Mint in Philadelphia, first inscribed on our coins the motto, "In God We Trust."

But one of the movement's most illustrious figures, who served as a manager and vice president from the time of the Union's inception until his death eighteen years later, once found himself held captive aboard a British ship outside the city of Baltimore, near Fort McHenry. He watched "the rockets red glare, the bombs bursting in air;" then he wrote *The Star Spangled Banner.*

Francis Scott Key, who taught a Bible class for boys, wrote another song in

1819. Though not widely known, it is still found in some hymnals:

Lord, with glowing heart I'd praise
Thee,
For the bliss Thy love bestows,
for the pardoning grace that saves
me,
And the peace that from it flows;
Help, O God, my weak endeavour;
This dull soul to rapture raise;
Thou must light the flame, or never
Can my love be warmed to praise.

Praise, my soul, the God that
sought thee,
Wretched wand'rer far astray;
Found thee lost, and kindly
brought thee
From the paths of death away;

Praise, with love's devoutest
feeling,
Him who saw thy guilt-born fear,
And, the light of hope revealing,
Bade the blood-stain'd cross
appear.

Praise the Saviour God that drew
thee,
To that cross, new life to give,
Held a blood-sealed pardon
to thee,
Bade thee look to him and live;
Praise the grace whose threats
alarmed thee,
Roused thee from thy fatal ease,
Praise the grace whose promise
warm'd thee,
Praise the grace that whispered
peace.

Lord, this bosom's ardent feeling
Vainly would my lips express;
Low before thy footstool kneeling,
Deign thy suppliant's pray'r
to bless;
Let thy love, my soul's chief
treasure,
Love's pure flame with me raise;
And since words can never
measure,
Let my life show forth thy praise.

And to a friend who was a member of Congress he once wrote:

"If you are convinced you are a sinner, that Christ alone can save you from

Paul and Sharon Hess (shown above with the President), youngest legislators in the Kansas state house, are known for their Christian convictions in the political arena.

the sentence of condemnation; if you make an unconditional surrender of yourself to His service, He will in no wise cast [you] out."

IN THE RANKS of America's leaders today are still those who recognize that the destiny of the nation must rest upon a strong Christian base.

Nebraska's Senator Carl Curtis, for instance, thinks the nation's basic problem is "theological, not political. It is lack of basic acceptance of simple Christian doctrine which is absent from many pulpits." Curtis believes the concept of separation of church and state has been "carried to ridiculous ends. The founding fathers simply didn't want a state religion such as England had. School authorities today think

they can't have a minister to give the invocation at graduation exercise ... What's wrong with public recognition that God exists?"

Folksy Tennessee congressman John Duncan, who often shows touring high school delegations through the Capitol, says, "I always take groups to the little prayer room off the rotunda and talk to them about the spiritual foundations of our country. I quote George Washington where he said, 'There is no government without morality, no morality without religion, and no religion without God.' Then I tell them about the Mayflower Compact. After returning home, they write back and say that this glimpse at America's spiritual heritage was what most impressed them in Washington."

**rue Christianity is very much alive
in this country. I see some
spectacular things going on . . ."**

New York's Jack Kemp, who called signals for the Buffalo Bills before coming to Congress in 1970, strikes a similar Christian tone and charges that today's situational ethics, which have helped to erode our moral base, are "nothing but an outgrowth of Hegel's dialectical theory of history." But Kemp is optimistic. "True Christianity is very much alive in this country. I see some spectacular things going on in my community, in New York State, and here in Washington."

Meanwhile, other men like Arizona Congressman John Conlan echo Kemp's concern. Conlan recalls "drifting into the socialist pattern" during his last year of undergraduate work at Northwestern University, before he went on to Harvard. Then he was "reborn through faith in Jesus Christ." That summer he traveled behind the Iron Curtain to "see what socialism was really like. I came back," he says, "with different conceptions about man and the universe."

Conlan sees "two basic philosophies worldwide. One starts with God and makes man the minor premise. The other starts with no god and makes man the major premise."

If there is any chance to make God the major premise in Washington or elsewhere, Christians like these, you can be sure, will make it happen. One example is Conlan's wife Irene, who has

New York Congressman Jack Kemp.

launched many Bible studies among Congressional wives and other Washington women. It was through one of these groups, in fact, that Julie Nixon Eisenhower, in her own words, "received Jesus Christ as Savior" in April, 1974.

No, it is not those who are forthright about their spiritual convictions, even in high places, who jeopardize the American democracy. Rather, it is those who would deny such freedoms, if not the very God of creation.

## CHAPTER ELEVEN

# THROUGH ALL THE EARTH ABROAD

THE CONTINENT OF AFRICA, south of the Sahara, contained about 20 million Christians in 1952. Today it has nearly 70 million, an increase of nearly 50 million in less than a quarter century! Nothing like it has been seen in Christian history. An article in *U. S. News and World Report* suggests that the majority of Africans may turn to Christianity by the close of the century.

In the past few years hundreds of thousands of Latin Americans have been converted by the gospel—especially in Brazil and Chile. And to the east in Asia, great spiritual movements have swept Indonesia, Taiwan and Korea.

What can explain this phenomenon? What are the origins of such a religious explosion in the world of the Twentieth Century?

The Church of Jesus Christ, of course, first exploded at Pentecost. The Book of Acts describes how the gospel spread through the Mediterranean world of the First Century, and then into Europe. But in later centuries the message would become garbled by the trappings of Romanism until the great Reformation, when again the message would spring forth in all its power and simplicity.

From the Reformation came a new missionary thrust—especially out of Great Britian, but also from Scandinavian countries, Germany and other parts of Europe. And some of the most strong-minded Christians staked out their claims in America.

Yet even in the early days of our nation, little of the non-English-speaking world had ever heard the gospel. It was dominant in Scandianavia and a major influence in the Netherlands and Switzerland. It shared the German States with Roman Catholicism.

Africa, except for its shoreline along the Mediterranean and tiny pockets in

West and South Africa, was a closed, unexplored continent. A few nominal Christians existed at the Cape of Good Hope.

China and East Asia contained only a handful of believers. Cannibals populated the Pacific Islands, and Australia was empty of Christians.

The Muslim countries had hardly seen an evangelical.

An entrenched Roman Catholic hierarchy held closed the door to Latin America.

Christians held a small foothold in India.

China was closed, Japan and Korea sealed off.

Yet in the century to come, evangelical missionaries would penetrate all of these lands and, in some cases, exert profound influence—especially in education.

By far the greatest flow of these missionaries would come from America. Even today the United States holds pre-eminence with the total evangelical missionary force estimated at 30,000.

Most Americans do not realize, however, that much of this missionary thrust originated at our colleges and universities—especially in times of revival and spiritual awakening.

One might first point way back to David Brainerd, a student at Yale when the First Great Awakening was sweeping New England. Somewhat of a rebel toward religion until his junior year, he did an abrupt about-face after a spiritual experience during "a walk in the woods." He soon dedicated himself to an unbelievably strenuous work among New England Indian tribes, despite his severe tuberculous. Brainerd saw many Indians converted. But only five years after his Yale turnabout, he died at the home of Jonathan Edwards, to whose lovely daughter Jerusha he was engaged to be married.

Soon after Brainerd died Jonathan Edwards published an account of the life of the young man, together with his diary. The book so revealed Brainerd's character and dedication that it became a powerful influence on many lives on behalf of missions—even to this day. As one historian put it, "David Brainerd dead was a more potent influence for the missionary cause in general than was David Brainerd alive."

Or look back to the now historic "haystack meeting" of 1806. New England's spiritual climate had fallen to low ebb. At Williams College in Massachusetts anti-Christian demonstrations had forced new converts to form a secret society. One summer afternoon of that year five students met in a maple grove for private prayer. A sudden thundershower drove them to shelter under a haystack. There they prayed about a plan to reach the unevangelized world with the message of Christ. The

shower proved brief, and as the sun broke through the clouds, one of them, Samuel J. Mills, gave the decisive word, "We can do it, if we will."

Most of these went on to a nearby seminary, where others joined Mills and the group, including Adoniram Judson. They successfully petitioned their denomination (Congregational) to form the American Board of Commissioners for Foreign Missions, first such movement of its kind in America. Soon other denominations followed suit. More than $40,000 in donations flowed into the board to send the would-be missionaries abroad. In February, 1812, the five young men set sail out of Salem, Massachusetts, for India.

On the long voyage, Adoniram Judson and Luther Rice, though sailing on different vessels, were converted to Baptist principles after diligently studying the Scriptures. The event seemed providential to Baptists in America. Judson went on to exercise a dramatic missionary impact in Burma; Rice came back to awaken Baptists in America to the missionary challenge.

The student awakening in New England touched off an indirect impact upon Hawaii, then a Polynesian kingdom in the North Pacific. A Hawaiian youth, Opukahaia (or Henry Obookiah), had found his way to Yale. Missionary zealot Samuel Mills took a keen interest in the young man, but one day Opukahaia died. The next year a party of missionaries, challenged by his untimely death, sailed for Hawaii.

The party expected to find the worst in degradation, but upon landing in 1820 they discovered that Christianity spreading from the islands of Tahiti and Tonga (where the British had planted the gospel a quarter century earlier) had already greatly modified Hawaiian paganism. The Hawaiian king granted the missionaries freedom to proceed, and in their first decade of work they won converts in the royal family and

Haystack prayer meeting

among the chiefs, established churches, influenced legislation that upgraded moral standards and educated thousands of children in schools (a somewhat different picture than that painted by modern-day novelists). A Hawaiian "Great Awakening" erupted in Hilo in 1837, and within five years more than twenty-seven thousand converts—a fifth of the entire population—were added to the churches.

Meanwhile, also as a result of spiritual awakening, British and Dutch missionaries moved northward from their base at Capetown, South Africa, to plant the gospel in the heart of Africa. Among now famous names in this effort were Robert Moffat and David Livingstone.

BACK IN THE UNITED STATES, spiritual life declined in the 1840's and 1850's as contentions over the slavery issue diverted energies. Also, the emergence of such cults as the Millerites (Jehovah's Witnesses) helped undermine religion's credibility when their predictions of Christ's return failed to materialize either in 1843 or in 1844. On campus, Greek letter fraternities replaced Christian groups. And many people were caught up in the financial prosperity which blossomed as the nation expanded westward.

Then came the revival of 1857-58. It started in New York when groups of office workers began to meet for prayer in churches and in theatres throughout lower Manhattan. These informal prayer meetings began to produce a growing stream of converts, and by May of 1858 newspapers in the city estimated the number of converts at 96,000. News media across the country reported the happening, as lesser publicized awakenings began in other states. It spread from the cities to the small towns and villages across the country, adding one million people to the nation's churches in just a year's time. Would-be critics could find no basis for charging fanaticism or hysteria. Clearly it had been a laymen's movement.

Since the revival started in New York and seemingly emerged simultaneously with the Wall Street bank panic of 1857-58, some historians have tried to link the two. But the former had begun before the economic crisis; it could not have "produced" the revival. And one analyst shrewdly points out that the 1929 crash produced no such event.

Moreover, a similar awakening occurred in Great Britain about the same time, then in South Africa, first among the Zulus, then among the English-speaking settlers. In the Zulu and Shosa tribes it triggered "an era of education." One South African historian declared that "the mid-century Awakenings certainly prepared the South African Bantu nations for their leading place in educational achievement in all of Africa, in primary as well as higher educa-tion."

As in previous revivals, American colleges felt the impact. The YMCA movement, then quite active on campus, helped reinforce it. The revival spread through Yale, Princeton and the other schools of New England, out to the University of Michigan and down into the schools of the South. It also spawned new colleges, such as The College of California out in Berkeley, established "to augment the discourse of reason, intelligence and faith." Later taken over by the state, it became the University of California.

Since the revival was not confined to America alone, neither was its missionary impact. From the American side, for instance, missionary pioneer William Taylor, moved by the awakening in California, took some of its effect to Australia and New Zealand. British, Scottish and Dutch missionaries pushed up into Central and East Africa, particularly into Uganda.

The revivals sent many medical missionaries to India from both Europe and America. Even as late as World War II, a survey in India revealed the evangelical impact: ninety percent of all nurses throughout India were Anglo-Indian or Indian Christians, most of them trained at mission hospitals. In those pockets of India where missionaries worked, they also made a great contribution to Indian agriculture still evident today. Had the pentration of Christian missionaries there been deeper and more widespread, the spectre of hunger facing that country today might be far less severe.

Protestant missionaries also headed for China, opened Japan and established some tiny footholds in Latin America. Evangelical Christian soldiers from the Army of the Confederacy established an educational work in Brazil that became the forerunner of the Brazilian educational system.

When Argentine President Domingo F. Sarmiento—educator, journalist and author—completely reorganized his country's educational system in the late 1860's, he personally enlisted some sixty-five dedicated school teachers from the United States. Sixty of these were evangelicals. Twenty-five years later Argentine literacy had climbed from 20 to 50 percent as a result of the normal schools that the Americans established.

JUMP NOW TO 1886 and a conference of 250 collegians at Mount Hermon, Massachusetts. Evangelist Dwight L. Moody had put the event together, prompted by Princeton student Luther Wishard and Moody's own growing interest in campus evangelism following his mission to Cambridge and several Ivy League schools.

Robert P. Wilder, head of the stu-

dent foreign missions movement at Princeton, showed up, talking about the call to missions to anyone who would listen. Wilder had been praying that a thousand students from American universities might be enlisted for foreign missionary enterprise. He persuaded Moody to set aside some time in the conference's loose program to focus on missions. The talks and the prayers that resulted prompted one-hundred delegates to sign a declaration indicating they would be willing to serve overseas. Wilder and a Princeton classmate, John Forman, then toured the universities enlisting some two-thousand volunteers. By the following year that number had swelled to three thousand. Forman crossed the Atlantic to extend the same challenge to the universities in the British Isles.

So originated the Student Volunteer Movement for Foreign Missions, which took as its motto, "the evangelization of the world in this generation." Cornell student John R. Mott was appointed

**The years of missionary groundwork—
much of it from America—
are beginning to pay off.**

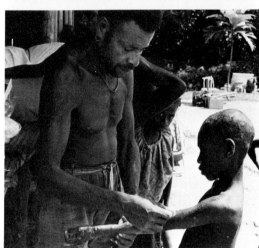

chairman, a position he would hold for more than thirty years. The late Yale Professor Kenneth Scott Latourette, greatest of the church historians, affirmed that this movement recruited and sent forth a large proportion of the outstanding leaders in the spread of Protestant Christianity abroad.

Spiritual awakenings around the world marked the first few years of the Twentieth Century. The astounding Welsh Revival of 1904 swept one-hundred-thousand persons into the churches in Wales in just three months and completely transformed the moral climate of that land. In Australia and New Zealand, one-fourth of all college students were members of the Christian Student Movement, and one-sixth were enrolled in Bible classes. Revival was seen in Scandinavia, Germany, South Africa.

It came to the United States in 1905, first in the Welsh mining towns of Pennsylvania, then spreading to New York, Atlantic City, Philadelphia, Atlanta, Los Angeles. Denver proclaimed a day of prayer and, at the mayor's request, closed its schools and almost all businesses. Twelve-thousand people crowded the churches and theatres for noon prayer.

It swept through almost all the major colleges, among them Northwestern University, Stanford, the University of Michigan. Again it spawned new schools, among them the Bible Institute of Los Angeles (now Biola College). And it accelerated the missionary movement, sending hundreds to the foreign field before the onset of war and revolution that would keep the world in turmoil for decades. Among these volunteers was T. J. Bach, who would later direct The Evangelical Alliance Mission.

Then there was William Borden of Yale, a young millionaire converted in the revival, who threw himself with abandon into the missions scene. He founded the Yale Hope Mission, a skid-row project, then volunteered for service with the China Inland Mission. In Egypt he mastered Arabic, which proved useful in China's great northwest. Though he lost his life, his example lingered to recruit men and women for China and other missions abroad.

As the universities grew and became so thoroughly secularized, the sources of missionary recruits in the Twentieth Century shifted more to the Bible institutes and Christian colleges—schools like Moody Bible Institute, Wheaton

By many means missionaries
are bringing the Gospel to the world.

College and many others. But not entirely. The nation's secular colleges and universities, whether intentionally or not, still turn out far more missionaries-in-the-making than the public realizes.

Such modern-day student movements as Inter-Varsity Christian Fellowship contribute immensely to this phenomenon. Fourteen thousand attended Inter-Varsity's gigantic week-long missionary conference at the University of Illinois between Christmas and New Year's eve, 1973. (Seventeen thousand are expected in 1976). Students from across the United States and abroad sacrifice a week at home with their families to hear the challenge of world-wide missions, to meet daily in small groups for Bible study and prayer, to attend workshops, to talk with more than one hundred mission

exhibitors about careers, and, yes, to pursue even yet "the evangelization of the world in this generation."

Meanwhile, scores of mission agencies, large and small, press forward with new vigor, new vision, new expertise. Some missionaries strategize for the evangelization of whole continents, while others work quietly in remote towns and villages. Some work among the professional class, others the students or the elite, while yet others bury themslves in the jungle painstakingly translating the Bible into an obscure tribal tongue. Yet all is toward one purpose, because Jesus commanded his followers to go and "teach all nations." The gospel is for all men, everywhere, and throughout all generations. "For God so loved the *world* ...

Today mission groups use all the modern technology at hand. Missionary

Flags of many nations—a reminder that the gospel is for all men.

pilots fly daily into remote, once inaccessible jungles. Powerful radio transmitters beam the gospel into Soviet Russia, where religion refuses to die, and into Red China, where no missionary can go. Evangelicals continue to pour food, Bibles, medicine, into areas of great need. And at the Missions Advanced Research Center (MARC) in Pasadena, California, a computor spits out the latest figures on unreached tribes, and pinpoints geographical areas of response as missionary strategists eagerly look for evidence of new Christian advance.

World evangelization may seem an

impossible task, and indeed much of the world remains unreached. But exciting events have begun to unfold. Today's missionary momentum is shifting into the hands of those in the Third World, and this is as it should be. Latin America, Africa and Asia not only are training their own people to evangelize, but they are also sending missionaries to other countries. The years of missionary groundwork—much of it from America—are beginning to pay off. The gospel explodes forth.

Anyone who grasps the flow of history and the purposes of God will sense America's role in this divine world plan: the remarkably late discovery of the continent itself, the unique Christian foundations, the revivals which sent forth from this land the seeds for spiritual revolution among other peoples of the earth.

Such truth, though, leaves no room for feelings of American superiority. The gospel cuts across all national boundaries. It also jumps the barriers of age, race, social class, education. The apostle Paul, a highly educated man, saw himself as "debtor both to the Greeks and to the barbarians; both to the wise and to the unwise" (Rom. 1:14). He knew the gospel was for both the cultured and the uncultured, the educated and the uneducated. Jesus declared that the gospel must first be preached among all nations (Mark 13:10). In Romans the apostle Paul speaks of "obedience to the faith among all nations, for his name" (Rom. 1:5). The same theme reappears in the final chapter (Rom 16:26). God indeed today is calling out a people for his name—from "every kindred, and tongue, and people, and nation" (Rev. 5:9).

Oh, for a thousand tongues to sing
Thy great redeemer's praise,
To spread through all the earth abroad
The honors of Thy name.

Jesus Christ is the Man for all men. This leaves no place for cultural snobbishness, smug isolationism or racial prejudice. Christianity is not simply "the white man's religion."

But it should never cease to excite true Christians of America that we are involved in a magnificent worldwide plan and cause.

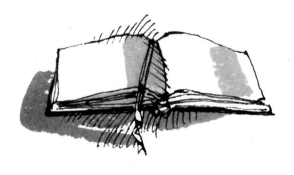

CHAPTER TWELVE

# GOD SHED HIS GRACE ON THEE

NOT LONG AFTER the United States became a nation, French political philosopher Alexis de Tocqueville visited America to search for that quality of greatness that had enabled a handful of people to defeat the mighty British Empire.

He looked for that greatness in our harbors and rivers, our fertile fields and boundless forests, our mines and natural resources. He studied our schools, our Congress and our Constitution, without finding the real answers.

It was not, he says, until he went into the churches of America and heard the pulpits "aflame with righteousness" that he could put his finger on the secret of our strength. Alexis de Tocqueville returned to France and wrote this warning: "America is great because America is good, and if America ever ceases to be good, America will cease to be great."

As an outside observer he sensed that America's destiny would depend on those inner qualities which make a nation great and upon strong moral foundations. What he admired in her people rested heavily on Christian foundations.

We may find qualities to admire in any man, be he Christian or otherwise. And every citizen, regardless of faith, either strengthens or weakens the character of a nation. But can it be mere coincidence that the most blessed nation on earth has, over the years, also been so evangelical? So much so, in fact, that it has come to be known as a "Christian" nation.

Yet strictly speaking, by the Bible's own definition, many Americans are not "Christians."

No, instead they have simply absorbed the "Christian" culture, however short that culture may fall from its ideal or potential.

They live under a "Christian" form of government that many feel most closely achieves the biblical ideal—one that has protected our freedoms and served America well for two hundred years, despite those who would sometimes abuse it.

They assent to "Christian" ideals, or to a Christian creed, or perhaps even attend a "Christian" church (which may or may not preach the gospel in clarity, depending upon the theological bent of the pastor).

But too often they lack a personal knowledge of the Scriptures or of the Savior.

It was not so with many of the early settlers, who knew the reality of salvation and the Bible's application to daily life. Millions since that time have come and gone with the same assurance. But like Israel of old, the spiritual tides of America sometimes ebb and sometimes flow. At this hour personal religion seems to be on the upsurge. Too many have known the emptiness of mere religion without Jesus Christ.

As one prominent United States Senator put it after his conversion some years ago, "I came to see that one became a Christian not by relationship to an organization, but by relationship to a Person, Jesus Christ."

The Scriptures teach, of course, that God will judge both nations and individuals. But he is also a God of grace.

At the personal level, God extends his grace to all those who will come to Him. It is a "grace far greater than all our sins." "My grace is sufficient for thee" (2 Corninthians 12:9), says our Lord, and where sin abounds, grace

**Jesus Christ is the Man for all time.**

does much more abound (see Rom. 5:20). "God is able to make all grace abound toward you ..." (2 Cor. 9:8). And "by grace are ye saved through faith, not by works, lest any man should boast" (Eph 2:8-9).

At the national level, God withholds judgment when people turn to Him. "If my people, which are called by my name, shall humble themselves, and pray, and seek my face, and turn from their wicked ways; then will I hear from heaven, and will forgive their sin, and will heal their land." (2 Chron. 7:14). Several times in the history of our nation widespread revival has put God's people back on course. Each time it has reversed a downward moral trend in society and ultimately unleashed profound social impact.

Such is the dynamic of men and

women empowered by the Jesus Christ who suffered agonizing death, who spilled blood at Calvary for man's sin and guilt, and who then burst forth from the grave.

When Jesus Christ came to Earth, He made available a grace that would extend through history to all who would respond.

Two-thousand years now have passed. A supersonic jet screams across the Atlantic in less time than it took the wise men to feed and water their camels. Thirteen men have kicked up dust on the same moon which helped illumine the fields as the shepherds watched over their flocks by night. An unmanned satellite races toward a distant planet whose twinkling light faintly penetrated that dark, agonizing night in the Garden of Gethsemane. There the

One who sweat great drops of blood moved deliberately toward the Cross and changed the course of history. Our beginnings reach back far beyond Paul Revere and a bicentennial, for Christ died seventeen centuries before the United States were born.

Why should the Jesus of those days so long ago have any appeal to our modern generation?

The Palestine of Jesus' day and our Twentieth Century scene may seem to be worlds apart. But sin hasn't changed. God hasn't changed. Jesus Christ hasn't changed—neither His judgment nor His love. And the same Holy Spirit of Pentecost is at work on earth in the lives of people today—across America and abroad.

Our Savior, of course, never was and

never will be confined to time, for His existence is eternal. Unlike all other religious leaders of world history, He came to Earth from outside this planet. He, whose goings forth have been from of old, from everlasting (Mic. 5:2). He was "with the Father before the world was" (John 17:4). And so will He be forevermore. "I am Alpha and Omega, the beginning and the ending, saith the Lord, who is, and who was, and who is to come, the Almighty" (Rev. 1:8).

In Him lie all the secrets of the universe, the origin of life, the direction of history, the life beyond.

Abraham Lincoln must have realized some of these truths when he spoke of the "Almighty Architect," the "Ruler of the Universe," the "God of Nations." Without at least an elementary grasp of God's sovereign hand behind all history, which our founding fathers so clearly understood, modern Americans will overlook the true meaning of their own land. If some from the older generations have missed it, then let the new generation know now the mighty sweep of spiritual events in our heritage and the story of how, and when, and why "God shed His grace on thee."

# SOURCES

## CHAPTER ONE

Appel, Fredric C., "The Coming Revolution in Transportation," condensed from *National Geographic*, September 1969.

Hatfield, Mark O., "The Shadow of Global Hunger," *Moody Monthly*, January 1975, page 31.

Phillips, John McCandlish, "Will the Real Christian Please Stand Up!" *Moody Monthly*, April 1971, pages 21-22.

Sweeting, Dr. George, "America, Right or Wrong?" *Moody Monthly*, July-August 1974, page 3.

Wattenberg, Ben J., "Let's Dispel the Gloom," *Christian Life*, July-August 1975, page 22.

## CHAPTER TWO

Flood, Robert, "Ten Events That Changed Christian History," *Moody Monthly,* October 1964, pages 26ff.

Hall, Verna M., compiler, *The Christian History of the Constitution,* Foundation for American Christian Education, San Francisco, 1973.

Huestis, Ruth Terhune, "Miracle on the Mayflower," *Moody Monthly*, November and December 1970, pages 32ff (Nov.) and pages 10ff (Dec.).

Kling, August John, "The Christopher Columbus That Few People Knew," *Moody Monthly*, October 1972, pages 27ff. Originally published in *Presbyterian Layman*.

Morison, Samuel Eliot, "Christopher Columbus, Mariner," *American Heritage*, December 1955, pages 72-95.

## CHAPTER THREE

Hall, Verna M., compiler, *The Christian History of the Constitution,* Foundation for American Christian Education, San Francisco, 1973, pages 151ff, 176ff and 262-269.

Russell, Francis, "Apostle to the Indians," *American Heritage,* December 1957, pages 4-9 and 117-119.

Sweet, William Warren, *The Story of Religion in America*, Harper & Row, Publishers, Inc., New York, 1950.

## CHAPTER FOUR

Campbell, Tim J., *Central Themes of American Life*, Wm. B. Eerdmans Publishing Co., Grand Rapids, Michigan, 1959.

Hall, Verna M., compiler, *The Christian History of the Constitution*, Foundation for American Christian Education, San Francisco, 1973, pages 332, 380-390.

Hitt, Russell T., editor, *Heroic Colonial Christians*, adapted from "John Witherspoon: Son of Liberty" by Henry W. Coray. Copyright 1966 by J. B. Lippincott Company. Reprinted by permission of J. B. Lippincott Company.

Fleming, Thomas, "Washington's Prayer at Valley Forge." Reprinted with permission from the February 1974 *Reader's Digest*. Copyright 1974 by The Reader's Digest Association, Inc., pages 110ff.

Gaustad, Edwin Scott, *A Religious History of America*, Harper & Row, Publishers, Inc., New York, 1966.

Sweet, William Warren, *The Story of Religion in America*, Harper & Row, Publishers, Inc., New York, 1950.

## CHAPTER FIVE

Hall, Verna M., compiler, *The Christian History of the Constitution,* Foundation For American Christian Education, San Francisco, 1973.

Hitt, Russell T., editor, *Heroic Colonial Christians*, J. B. Lippincott Company, Philadelphia, 1966, pages 13-103.

## CHAPTER SIX

Sweet, William Warren, *The Story of Religion in America,* Harper & Row, Publishers, Inc., New York, 1950, page 215. Used by Permission. Also, pages 228-229, from a letter of the Rev. John Evans Finley, a Presbyterian minister in Kentucky, dated September 10, 1801, published in the New York Missionary Magazine (1802).

Teeter, Herman B., "The Incredible Francis Asbury, *Together* Magazine, August-September 1971, pages 27-36. Copyright 1971 by The Methodist Publishing House. Used by permission.

Weisberger, Bernard A., "Pentecost in the Backwoods," *American Heritage*, June 1959, page 81.

Whaley, Howard, "Three Little Churches and How They Grew," *Moody Monthly*, July-August 1966, pages 39-42.

## CHAPTER SEVEN

Johnstone, William J., *How Lincoln Prayed,* The Abingdon Press, Nashville, Tennessee, 1931, pages 57-58, 41-42 and 75-76.

Macartney, Clarence E., *Lincoln and the Bible*, Abingdon-Cokesbury Press, Nashville, Tennessee, 1949, page 5. Used by permission.

Sandburg, Carl, *Abraham Lincoln: The Prairie Years And The War Years,* one volume edition, Harcourt Brace Jovanovich, Inc., 1931. Used by permission.

## CHAPTER EIGHT

Miller, Basil, *Ten Famous Evangelists,* Zondervan Publishing House, Grand Rapids, Michigan, 1949.

Pollock, J. C., *Moody: A Biographical Portrait of the Pacesetter in Modern Mass Evangelism,* The Macmillan Company, 1963.

## CHAPTER NINE

Harrington, Anne, "The Youngest Legislators in Kansas," *Moody Monthly*, April 1975, pages 28ff.

Hefley, James C., and Edward E. Plowman, *WASHINGTON: Christians in the Corridors of Power,* Tyndale House Publishers, Inc., Wheaton, Illinois, 1975, pages 48, 59, 61-62. Used by permission.

Hefley, Marti, "Quiet Witness in Washington," *Moody Monthly*, January 1975, pages 24ff.

Moore, John N., "Another Choice," *Decision,* January 1975, page 3.

*U.S. News and World Report,* "Boom in Protestant Schools," October 8, 1973, pages 44-46 and "Pursuit of Happiness," August 27, 1973, pages 34-40.

## CHAPTER TEN

Flood, Robert G., "Who Is Undermining the Constitution?" *Moody Monthly*, October 1964, pages 1, 2.

Hefley, James C. and Edward E. Plowman, *WASHINGTON: Christians in the Corridors of Power,* Tyndale House Publishers, Inc., Wheaton, Illinois, 1975, pages 107ff. Used by permission.

Hefley, James C., *America: One Nation Under God,* Victor Books, Copyright 1975 by Scripture Press Publications, Inc., Wheaton, Illinois.

## CHAPTER ELEVEN

Orr, J. Edwin, *Campus Aflame*, Regal Books Division, Gospel Light Publications, Glendale, California, 1971.

## CHAPTER TWELVE

Flood, Robert G., "The Man For All Time and All Nations," *Moody Monthly,* December 1974, pages 24ff.

# PHOTO AND ART CREDITS

All continuity art by Tom Fawell

ROBERT FLOOD is Publication Director of *Moody Monthly*, coordinating the overall operations of America's fastest-growing Christian family magazine with a circulation exceeding one quarter million. From 1968-71 he served as Managing Editor. He graduated in 1958 with a B.S. in journalism from California State Polytechnic University, San Luis Obispo, where he edited their campus newspaper. After two years with the US Army the author studied at Moody Bible Institute, Chicago, and joined *Moody Monthly* in 1961.

★ ★ ★

TOM FAWELL, an award-winning illustrator, is President of American Motivate, Inc. and is a US history buff. He attended both the Art Institute in Chicago and Pratt Institute in New York. The New York Society of Illustrators recognized him for outstanding work in illustration. Tom Fawell and his team provide the graphic design for *Moody Monthly*.